Another Adventure in the Kingdom™

THE YOUNG GOD CHASERS

Seeker's SECRET PLACE

A Children's Church Experience
13-Week Curriculum

Dian Layton

With Quotes and Concepts from *Secret Sources of Power*
by T.F. Tenney and Tommy Tenney

Character illustrations by Al Berg.

Published by Mercy Place Ministries

MercyPlace is a licensed imprint of Destiny Image® Inc.

Distributed by

Destiny Image® Publishers, Inc.
P.O. Box 310
Shippensburg, PA 17257-0310

ISBN 0-9707919-2-5

For Worldwide Distribution
Printed in the U.S.A.

This book and all other Destiny Image, Revival Press, MercyPlace, Fresh Bread, Destiny Image Fiction, and Treasure House books are available at Christian bookstores and distributors worldwide.

To order books, call **1-800-722-6774.**
For more information on foreign distributors, call **717-532-3040.**
Or reach us on the Internet: **www.seeker.org**

THE YOUNG GOD CHASERS
Seeker's SECRET PLACE
Contents

THE YOUNG GOD CHASERS
Seeker's SECRET PLACE
Contents and Lesson Synopsis

Scripture Reference   Page

© 2003 Dian Layton

THE YOUNG GOD CHASERS
Seeker's SECRET PLACE
Contents and Lesson Synopsis

THE YOUNG GOD CHASERS
Seeker's SECRET PLACE
Contents and Lesson Synopsis

Introducing the Chase...

We highly recommend that you read *Secret Sources of Power* by T.F. Tenney and Tommy Tenney (Shippensburg, PA: Fresh Bread, an imprint of Destiny Image, 2000). Allow the Lord to settle the principles and concepts from the book in your own heart and then pray that He will instill them into the hearts of the children. It is also recommended that every person in your children's ministry read *Soldiers With Little Feet* by Dian Layton in order to really understand the philosophy behind this material.

Every lesson is written in a 90-minute time frame. This includes approximately 30 minutes for small groups—a major emphasis in this curriculum. If you have less time than 90 minutes, one suggestion is to split each lesson in half, thus taking 26 weeks to complete the material. If you have more time, extend the praise and worship sections and Small Group Time.

One main goal of this curriculum is for children to be established in a Kingdom lifestyle. It is not just learning about, but actually experiencing living for King Jesus and allowing Him to live through us!

Helpers for the Chase

PRAYER SUPPORT

This curriculum will be most effective in the lives of the children when it is covered in prayer! **Ask your church to PRAY for the YOUNG GOD CHASERS 13-Week Experience.** If your fellowship has small groups that meet regularly, communicate with them about prayer needs and give them testimonies of what God has been doing as the children chase Him!

KIDS IN MINISTRY OPPORTUNITY!

Throughout the curriculum are specially marked places where children can participate in an acting role or in some area of leadership. We do not want the children to be spectators, watching teens and adults do everything. These meetings are theirs—and we want them to take ownership and responsibility. **In addition to the specially marked places, watch for other areas to involve the children:**

- Singing and playing instruments
- Running sound
- Placing overhead transparencies
- Ushering and greeting
- Reading the Scriptures
- Leading a small group

This is a "Kids In Ministry Opportunity!"

Also involve the children in the corporate meetings in your main sanctuary. Give them opportunities to usher, take the offering, read Scriptures, pray, and sing on the worship team—even if it's just for one song!

Helpers for the Chase *continued*...

LEADER (of the Chase)

This person is the overseer of the meeting. It is his/her job to keep everything flowing and moving forward; to lead the children on each week's chase. There are written suggestions to facilitate this, but these are meant only to be guidelines. Key points are bolded for you. NOTE: Watch for extra opportunities throughout the lessons to review memory verses and truths learned in previous weeks. The LEADER of the Chase needs to be sensitive to the Holy Spirit. He/she must recognize when the Lord wants to do something and LET HIM do so! If at all possible, the LEADER should commit to leading all 13 weeks.

NOTE: The PRAYERparation Page at the beginning of each lesson is for YOU! It is the most important tool we've supplied for you to teach this curriculum. It is the foundation, the starting point. **Take time early in the week** to read it, look up the verses, and ask King Jesus to bring each week's theme alive to you. It must first be alive and real in your own heart before you will really be able to impart it to the children. Second Corinthians 3:6 in the *God Chasers Extreme New Testament* says: "He made us able ministers of a new agreement, which is spiritual, not literal. The letter of the law kills, but the Spirit gives life!" This is so important! Please spend time with King Jesus, letting His Spirit bring His Word for the children alive to you so that you do not offer dead, lifeless meetings to the children in your church!

NOTE: At the beginning of each lesson is the section: LEADER & SMALL GROUP LEADERS: PRAY FOR THE CHILDREN. Each week's prayer is based on a Scripture passage. Pray God's Word out loud, declaring it and claiming it! Pray it alone as part of your PRAYERparation time. Pray it again when you meet with the Small Group Leaders ten minutes before the children come into the room. You might also want to repeat the prayer as an opening to the meeting.

SONG LEADER

The song leader must love to praise and worship God. He/she also needs to understand how to reach children and have them focus on God and not themselves. He/she can be an adult or teen. Involve children by having them sing into microphones or play instruments.

KINGDOM RUNNER

The KINGDOM RUNNER *(who teaches most of the memory verses Weeks #1-5)* needs to be animated and energetic. KINGDOM RUNNER comes running in, wearing workout clothing. He runs around the room, then comes to the front and motions for the children to stand and begin running on the spot. "Hello, Young God Chasers! How is your chase going? Are you running toward King Jesus with all your heart?! While you are chasing God, you get strength from His presence...strength from the SECRET PLACE. It's an amazing place where you can live and rest and run—all at the same time!"

SPIRIT-MAN

The character SPIRIT-MAN is symbolic of our inner man—the part of us that was born again and came to life when we received Jesus as our Savior; the part of us that grows as we feed on God's Word and prayer. *(See Ephesians 3:16; 1 Peter 2:2.)* SPIRIT-MAN appears in this curriculum in one skit and once as a memory verse teacher. Have the letters SPIRIT-MAN put on the front of a white T-shirt. Have a shiny cape made of white, gold, or blue fabric and have a coordinating eye mask.

IMPORTANT NOTE: if you are short on personnel, ONE PERSON can be

The LEADER of the Chase, the SONG LEADER and teach the MEMORY VERSES!

Helpers for the Chase *continued*...

 CANDY RAPPERS

This is a group of energetic and extremely "cool" CHEERLEADERS throughout Weeks #2 to #5. Attach candy wrappers to their clothing and have them lead the cheer in a "rap" style. *(Idea: wear matching t-shirts.)*

KINGDOM ADMIRAL

The KINGDOM ADMIRAL teaches the memory verses Weeks #6-11. He/she needs to be animated and energetic, and speak in a commanding voice. Costume could be as simple as a sailor hat or as elaborate as a high-ranking naval officer can get! Every week's intro is the same: "Sailors—-please stand at attention as we read from the King's Great Book! Then we shall learn today's royal memory verse from the Hugga-Wugga™ Paraphrase!"

KINGDOM SAILORS

This is a group of energetic and extremely happy CHEERLEADERS throughout Weeks #6-11. They always enter running, wearing white sailor caps and doing sailor jig actions to the cheer. *(Example: right hand over right eye while hopping on right foot; then left.)* NOTE: The KINGDOM ADMIRAL could be the leader of the KINGDOM SAILORS.

Sing-A-Story-Theatre with the KING'S TRAVELING MUSICIANS

For Weeks #6-9, and 11 there are three "comedian-types" who sing a story each week about David. Although the stories have a strong message, the musicians themselves are quite ridiculous. They should have as much fun as possible—especially when making their entrances and exits. Each week they dress and act differently. A list of props and costume ideas is supplied.

SMALL GROUP LEADERS

Include grandparents, young adults, teens, or older children as you recruit Small Group Leaders. Teens and older children must be mature, responsible, reliable, and set a good example for the children.

Ask people to commit to the entire 13 weeks OR have two teams of group leaders, each serving six weeks in a row, and everyone coming to the Week #13 FAMILY ADVENTURE.

These people are not to teach! They are simply to CARE about the children and look at their group as their own little flock to shepherd and nurture. Their role is to facilitate discussion—not to do all the talking. **Make sure each Small Group Leader has the weekly Small Group outline page ahead of time so they can get "pre-prayered"!**

Elements of the Chase

SECRET PLACE TIME

Throughout the curriculum are places where the children can experience spending time with King Jesus in the SECRET PLACE. The LEADER of the Chase needs to be sensitive to the Holy Spirit and let HIM be the ultimate Leader! The goal of this curriculum is not to get through a lot of material and entertain the children—it is to facilitate a real EXPERIENCE with the King of kings.

It is definitely an ADVENTURE—because the King may do things differently than what you might have planned. Prayerfully review the suggestions for each SECRET PLACE TIME. Be prepared to let God interrupt at any point in the meeting. Let the King have His way!

*This curriculum places a lot of emphasis on giving our burdens over to the Lord. The prayer and expectation behind the lessons is that the children will **open their hearts up to God and let out the pain**. Our prayer is that they will DO what they learn, and that they will continue to walk in forgiveness and healing into their adult lives. What many children desperately need is a safe place where they can run into the arms of God and **unload their heavy burdens**. They need to cry, without having an adult telling them to stop. Throughout this curriculum, there are times in the SECRET PLACE when the children are encouraged to do just that. Will you help facilitate this? Will you provide a place, an atmosphere, where the children can spend **unhurried and unhindered time with King Jesus**?*

Here are some ideas to help you get the children to focus during SECRET PLACE TIME:

- **"Shhh!"**
  Teach the children that whenever you say that, they are to respond by saying, "Go into the SECRET PLACE!"

- **"1-2-3 Seek the King!" (OR "1-2-3 Chase God!")**
  Teach the children that whenever you say this, they are to very quickly find a chair to kneel at or a piece of floor to lie prostrate on. Past experience with children shows that a dimly lit room helps them to seek the King. So—one idea we've used is to first ask the children, "What time is it?" They respond with "It's time to seek the King!" Tell them to plan where they will seek Him….then count slowly, clearly, and with great anticipation: 1-2-3! Immediately, the lights go down, and everyone falls to their knees or on their face, praying loud, hard, and fast! This helps the children to focus on what they are doing and not be distracted by other children. You can vary this experience by telling them to whisper loud, hard, and fast; or to fall to their knees, lift their hands, and say nothing—just listen for God's voice.

- **Prayer Blankets**
  Children love to cozy up in a blanket. In this curriculum they will learn about the Holy Spirit, their Comforter. To reinforce the concept of being wrapped up in God's presence, we suggest having small blankets ready for each child to lie on or cover themselves with during the SECRET PLACE TIME. These can simply be 4' squares of inexpensive fabric cut out with pinking shears so the edges don't fray.

Elements of the Chase continued...

 ## SONGS (for the Chase)

Five new songs are included in this binder. We highly recommend that you USE these, as they will anchor the curriculum principles in the hearts of the children. One person may lead using the CD, or the worship time may be led by an entire team with live music! Words for the songs, as well as sheet music (melody line only) are in the back of the binder. The overhead transparencies can also be printed out directly from the CD.

Let children help lead the songs to provide a *This is a "Kids In Ministry Opportunity!"*

NOTE: Flashlights are a wonderful way to involve the children in worship. Hand out as many flashlights as possible——two for each child. Turn out the lights and lead in wide, easy actions to the music. This would be especially effective for the two songs "In the Secret Place" and "He Is My Hiding Place." Flashlights may be purchased at a dollar store; OR—if you like the idea of worshiping with flashlights, you may want to invest in higher quality flashlights and use them during events such as Christmas services.

If you have longer than 90 minutes with your group, you will probably want to extend the worship times and add songs the children are familiar with and which also support the theme. If you have done other YOUNG GOD CHASERS curriculum materials, intersperse those songs in each lesson.

NOTE: The song "Mommy, I Need You" is intended for use during the Week #13 FAMILY ADVENTURE. It is not intended to be one of the songs the children learn, thus we have not included it as an overhead transparency or in the sheet music.

MEMORY VERSES

The KINGDOM RUNNER (Weeks #1-5) and the KINGDOM ADMIRAL (Weeks #6-11) teach the weekly memory verses. SUGGESTION: a team of children could help teach *This is a "Kids In Ministry Opportunity!"* and review the verses each week. This would help to keep consistent voice inflection and actions.

Dian Layton, author of this curriculum, is also known as Hugga-Wugga™. To make memorization fun and easy, Dian teaches the H.W.P. (Hugga-Wugga™ Paraphrase) of Bible verses. To help you understand the rhythm of each verse, some words are printed in capital letters to show where to place emphasis, and there are corresponding actions. For a listing of all the verses, please refer to the back of the Introduction. Listen to the CD.

NOTE: Whoever teaches the verses MUST be prepared and lead with confidence in order to make sure they truly are POWER-FILLED verses! They must also be prepared each week to review previous verses.

Elements of the Chase continued...

CHEERS

The two cheers in this curriculum are taught by CANDY RAPPERS (Weeks #1-5) and the KINGDOM SAILORS (Weeks #6-11). These people should:

• Prepare actions, making sure they are simple for the children to learn.
• Recruit people of various ages to help and rehearse the cheers.
• Present the cheer each week and involve the children. Copy the CHEER onto an overhead transparency and use that to teach the words.

CREATIVE ILLUSTRATIONS

Throughout the curriculum are skits and a variety of creative teaching ideas. Most of these are VERY SIMPLE and require LITTLE OR NO REHEARSAL. The creative illustrations have suggested formats, but you can adapt each one to your setting—as rehearsed skits, spontaneous narrated skits, or shadow plays. Many of the scripts would be suitable for puppets.

Assign as many of the parts as possible to CHILDREN to provide them with a

This is a "Kids In Ministry Opportunity!"

IMPORTANT NOTE: The LEADER of the Chase or The KINGDOM RUNNER can cover many of these parts if you are short on personnel.

ALSO: many of the acting parts could easily be played by PUPPETS.

Make sure to look at scripts well in advance and hand out copies to your actors at least two weeks early. **Although most of the materials require little or no rehearsal, there are a few that will need some extra preparation.**

THROUGHOUT THE CURRICULUM

Assign a "Royal Photographer" to take pictures every week. Have these pictures ready to display on Week #13 for the FAMILY ADVENTURE—in photo albums, hanging on the wall, on overhead transparencies, or as a computer presentation.

• Leaders and helpers praying before the meeting

• Praise & worship time

• Skits

• Memory verses

• SECRET PLACE TIME

• Small Group time

• Behind the scenes

Elements of the Chase continued...

✠ SMALL GROUP

Small Groups are a very important part of the YOUNG GOD CHASERS Experience, and for this particular curriculum, they are VITAL. They are NOT a teaching time, but rather a type of children's "care group." Children need to feel like they belong. When new children visit your fellowship, they will be interested in the children's ministry program, but they will be MORE interested in whether or not they are accepted by the other children. Small Group Time is a regular, hands on way to involve the children of your church in a meaningful ministry opportunity. Encourage them to make new children feel welcome. Also encourage the children to really care for each other—to reach out to children who are going through hard times, etc. The Small Group Time is intended to facilitate an opportunity for discussion, prayer, and fellowship—all centered around the lesson.

Small Group will be something the children look forward to each week—a time when they know a caring person will be there to listen and be interested about what is important in their lives. **Your genuine care for each child will make an ETERNAL difference!!!!**

The groups can be divided up according to age, or you can mix the ages together. The ideal scenario would be to have enough God-chasing mature children, teens, adults, and/or older folks to oversee groups of four to eight children. If you do not have that many people, just try to keep groups as small as possible for ultimate effectiveness. Each leader should keep a supply bag with name tags and other necessary materials.

Make sure each Small Group Leader has the weekly Small Group outline page ahead of time so they can be "pre-prayered"!

SMALL GROUP PROCEDURE

#1 MEET AT THE BEGINNING OF THE LESSON *(Optional)*

Have the leaders come to the children's ministry room early to pray. When the children enter the room, they should be greeted at the door, then sent to the area of the room where their particular group is meeting. *(Or their designated row of seating.)* Take attendance and give the children name tags.

#2 SIT TOGETHER IN THE MEETING

The Small Groups should sit together throughout the meeting and have a "team" feel. The leaders should help the children find Scripture verses and encourage their participation in all parts of the meeting. They should model attentiveness and worship for their Small Group.

#3 SMALL GROUP TIME

At the end of every lesson the Small Groups sit together in their specific area of the room for prayer, discussion of the lesson, and looking up Scriptures. Have FUN looking up the Bible verses; and let the children offer their own paraphrased version of each one. **NOTE:** If you divide the children according to age, the leaders of the five- and six-year-olds will need to be resourceful in this area. Perhaps look up a verse in one child's Bible and read it aloud; the next verse in another child's Bible and so on.

Encourage the children to pray for each other's requests. Be sensitive to your particular group—some children will be confident in this, others will need time and encouragement to grow. **You may want to have regular prayer lists where each Small Group is assigned to pray for different aspects of church life each week.**

Each week if you have time, look up the Scripture passage and read the story from the Bible. Many children have heard the stories, but have never actually looked at the story in Scripture.

**DOOR-HANGERS: Each week a memory verse door-hanger
is provided for the children to cut out and take home. Encourage them
to use these each time they are spending time with King Jesus.**

LETTERS TO THE KING

Here are ideas for two different styles of "SHIP LETTER BOXES." During the SECRET PLACE TIME, in Small Groups, or in the corporate meeting, the children can express their feelings in the form of letters to the King. They can also bring letters they write during the week. The letters are confidential and the children need to know that no one will ever look at them—they are for the King only. The "SHIP LETTER BOXES" should be taken home at the end of the curriculum and still used by the children when they spend time in their SECRET PLACE.

"SHIP LETTER BOX" Suggestion #1

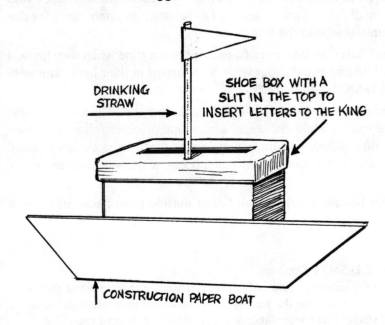

DRINKING STRAW

SHOE BOX WITH A SLIT IN THE TOP TO INSERT LETTERS TO THE KING

CONSTRUCTION PAPER BOAT

"SHIP LETTER BOX" Suggestion # 2 *(Enlarge attached pattern)*

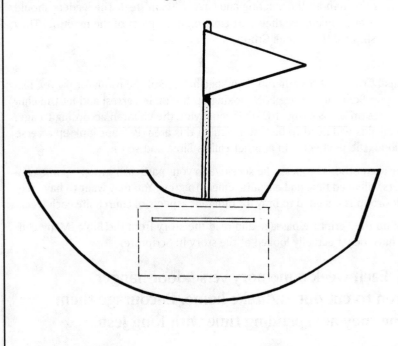

Paste an envelope on the reverse side of a construction paper boat. Cut a slot in boat where the children can insert their letters to the King each week. Label each child's letter boat and mount it on the wall as part of a display. The children take their letter boats home at the end of the curriculum.

"SHIP LETTER BOX" Suggestion #2 Pattern

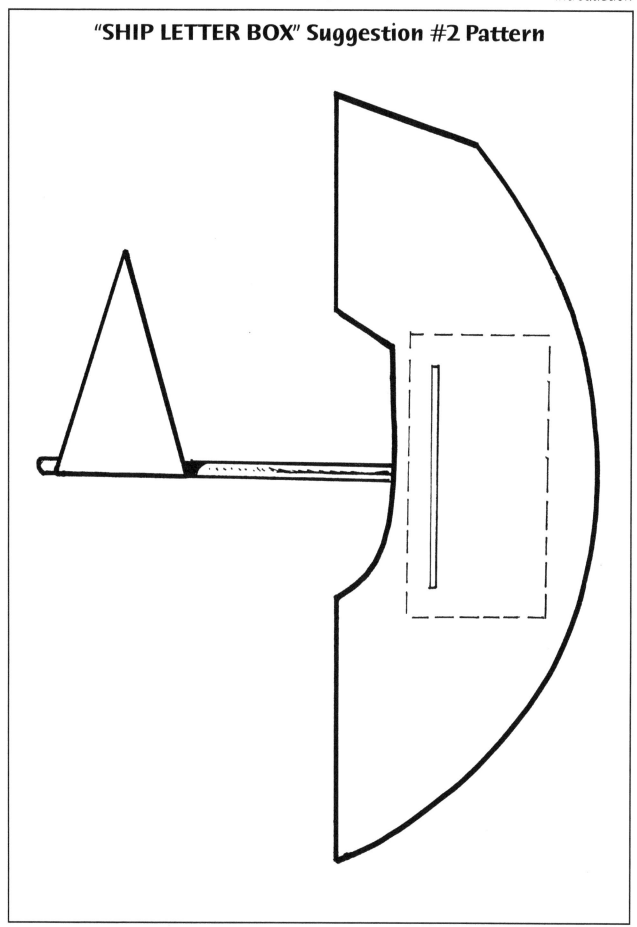

LOOKING AHEAD TO...
Week #12 - "PRAYERparation for the FAMILY ADVENTURE"

Note: Ask your pastor to come to the meeting today and speak some words of encouragement to the children and pray for them about next week's FAMILY ADVENTURE.

The focus of this week is to provide adequate time to pray and rehearse for next week's presentation in the sanctuary. But if you have enough time, you may want to have a small party this week; or you can use the following ideas at a later time.

SAILOR PARTY!

Paper boat hats for everyone to wear. *(Please refer to next page)*

ROYAL PHOTOGRAPHER should show pictures he/she has taken throughout the curriculum.

Serve snacks
Snack Ideas: Use a ship theme. Make little boats with cookies for the bases. Slightly warm a marshmallow so it is sticky and set it on the cookie. Insert a toothpick holding a flag cut from fruit roll-ups. Or just insert the toothpick flags into cupcakes. Also serve fish crackers and gummy worms. Drink blue Kool-Aid™.

Play Games
- Boat Race: Use children's wading pools and any style of toy boats. Have teams of children blow their boats in a race to the other side of the pool.

- Another kind of boat race: For each team, cut out a paper boat and thread it on a 13 foot long string. Stretch the string out and hang it on the wall. Using bright ribbons, mark each foot of length. Alternate between each group, asking them to say one of the 13 memory verse they have learned. If the verse is quoted accurately, their boat moves forward one foot.

- Balloon Boat Race: For each team thread about 30 feet of string through a drinking straw. Tie either end of the string to two heavy chairs and move them apart until the string is taut. Have the drinking straw at the chair where the race will begin. Blow up a balloon as large as possible and tie the end with a twist tie. Using a long piece of tape, attach the balloon to the drinking straw. Each team selects one person to untie the twist tie when the race begins. The team whose balloon boat reaches the other chair first is the winner.

  Note: Add a drinking straw mast with a flag to the balloon so it looks more like a boat.

Paper Boat Hats

Make these from rectangular-shaped paper. Newspaper works great!

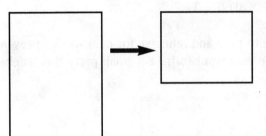

Step #1: Fold the paper in half, making a smaller rectangle.

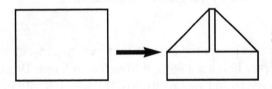

Step #2: Bring both folded corners into the center, making two triangular shapes.

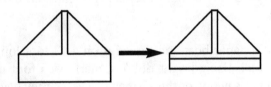

Step #3: Fold the lower edge up to meet the bottom of the folded triangles. Do the same on the reverse side.

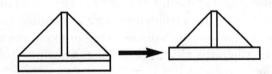

Step #4: Fold the lower edge up again, this time to overlap the folded triangles.

Step #5: Open the hat and put it on!

LOOKING AHEAD TO...
Week # 13 - "A FAMILY ADVENTURE"

Week #13's FAMILY ADVENTURE has powerful potential to bring healing to families in your church fellowship. Please aprroach it with PRAYER. Ask King Jesus for HIS plan. Read through the suggested outline, especially the section: "FAMILY PRAYER TIME in the SECRET PLACE." Listen to the song "Mommy, I Need You" on the CD. Be watching for children who have leadership skills to help lead the verses, songs, and cheers. Also watch for possible children to give a testimony to the congregation. You should add, delete, or expand the Week #13 suggested outline according to what King Jesus tells you, being sensitve to what your children are prepared to do, as well as the available time frame.

*You will want to request at least 45 minutes at the end of the service.

IMPORTANT:

Give a copy of the FAMILY ADVENTURE outline to your PASTOR.

Ask for his feedback and recommendations.

DO NOT lead the congregation in the FAMILY PRAYER TIME unless you have your pastor's release and blessing.

FAMILY MEAL

Suggestion: Have everyone stay after church that day for lunch. One idea would be to use the children's offering and pay to have lunch catered. (Choose a simple, inexpensive meal like lasagna and salad.) The goal would be to supply FAMILY time—so you would want to avoid having the moms in the kitchen! Perhaps you could have a group of single folks oversee the meal.

Suggestion: Have the children serve their parents. Or at least, have the children wait while their parents go through the line first!

*PLEASE NOTE: Pray and ask King Jesus if a family meal at church is what He wants. After families pray together that day, and the Lord is ministering to their hearts, it may very well be most appropriate just to let people go home.

Memory Verses - At a Glance

Week #1 - Psalms 91:1-2; Matthew 6:6

Memory Verse #1

WORDS	ACTIONS
"Kids who live in	*Hold up left forefinger*
the SECRET PLACE	*Right forefinger to lips and whisper*
of the Most High	*Point right forefinger up to Heaven*
(Most High)	*Right forefinger down then up again*
Have a place of rest in the Shadow of the King	*Bring right hand down to cover left forefinger and pull it gently to heart*
Psalm 91: 1	*Poke left forefinger up from behind right hand*
and 2	*Hold out two fingers of right hand*
God has a special home for you!	*Look down at right hand still over left forefinger at your heart*
In the SECRET PLACE….In the SECRET PLACE…"	*Keep hands the same and rock gently back and forth to the beat.*

Memory Verse #2

WORDS	ACTIONS
"Shhh!	*Right forefinger to lips*
Go into the SECRET PLACE	
And shut the door!	
Your heavenly Father hears your prayer	
He WILL reward!	
Matthew 6:6-	*Whisper and pat legs to the beat*
Say it till it STICKS!"	*Hands get "stuck" on legs until you finally pull them off abruptly*

Week #2 - Matthew 11:28

WORDS	ACTIONS
"Matthew 11:28—see—	*Hold both hands out to the side with palms upturned, chest height*
Jesus said, 'Come to ME	*Keep hands the same; wave fingers toward chest*
With your heavy burdens!	*Pull fists to heart and be weighed down with heavy burdens that pull you to the floor in a squatting position*
And I will give you rest…Ahh…	
And I will give you rest…Ahhhhh…	
And I—will give—you—rest…Ahhhhhhh…'"	*Get up gradually, pulling hands apart as the weight is lifted until at the end both hands are raised, totally free!*

Week #3 - Hebrews 12:1

WORDS	ACTIONS
	Run on the spot
"Get rid of anything that slows you down	*Continue to run while pulling off an invisible heavy coat*
And don't let SIN	*Forearms crossed at chest; make fists*
tie you up!	*Fist rotate over fist several times*
(Uh-uh!)	*Break free!*
Keep on running the race ahead	*Run on the spot with greater determination*
That's Hebrew 12, verse 1! (Uh-HUH!)	
That's Hebrew 12, verse 1! (Uh-HUH!)"	*Stretch - touching toes left, then right*

Week #4 - Matthew 6; Ephesians 4:32

Memory Verse #1

WORDS	ACTIONS
"From Matthew chapter 6: The Lord's Prayer…	*Look at an invisible open Bible you are holding*
and beyond…	*Look forward*

Week #4 - Matthew 6; Ephesians 4:32

Memory Verse #1, continued

WORDS	ACTIONS
Lord, forgive my sins in exactly the same way	*Turn slightly right; reach up with both hands and receive forgiveness from the Lord into your heart*
I choose to forgive other people."	*Turn slightly left; reach out with both hands and offer forgiveness to another person*

Memory Verse #2

WORDS	ACTIONS
"Be kind to one another	*With a partner—clap own hands, their hands, left, right, own and repeat to the beat.*
Tender-hearted	
Forgiving one another	
'Cause God's forgiven you!	
Ephesians 4	
verse-32!"	*Clap own hands then slap sides sharply*

Week #5 - John 7:38-39

WORDS	ACTIONS
"The Holy Spirit is a lot like a River	
Of water that is ALIVE!	*Country style! Both hands slightly in front pants*
Flow in and out of ME, Holy Spirit	*pockets and lean right then left on the beat and*
That's John chapter 7:38 and 39"	*speak with an exaggerated drawl.*

Week #6 - Phillipians 4:6

WORDS	ACTIONS
"Don't worry about ANYTHING—	*Both hands to temples and shake head*
Just BE THANKFUL!	*Hand over hand under chin; look up thankfully*
Don't worry about ANYTHING—	*Both hands to temples and shake head*
Just BE THANKFUL!	*Hand over hand under chin; look up thankfully*

Week #6 - Phillipians 4:6, continued

WORDS	ACTIONS
Tell Jesus what you want	*Flip left palm up*
tell Jesus what you need	*Flip right palm up*
Philippians chapter 4 verse 6—	*Bring both palms together at chest, gradually on beat*
Always, always be	*Slap hand under hand on beat*
THANKFUL! Be THANKFUL! Be THANKFUL!"	*Cup hand under hand and rock with exaggerated shoulder movements*

Week #7 - Psalms 61 and 62

WORDS	ACTIONS
"I love reading Psalms 61 and 62 When I'm in trouble, I know what to do! I run to the Rock and I pour out my heart	*Snap right then left on the beat*
I do run, run, run; I do run, run I do run, run, run; I do run, run—to the Rock!"	*Fist over fist right then left on the beat*

Week #8 - 1 Peter 5:7

WORDS	ACTIONS
"Casting all my cares upon Him—	*Hold imaginary fishing pole with both hands and "cast it" up and out toward Heaven*
Because Jesus cares for me!	*Let go of the pole and wave like waving cares good-bye*
Pouring out my heart in prayer—	*With both hands at chest "pour out" your heart as you kneel gradually*
My burdens are released! First Peter 5 verse 7—HEY!	*Pull fists to heart* *Jump up, pulling hands apart as the weight is lifted until at the end both hands are raised, totally free!*
Give your cares to Jesus	*Hold imaginary fishing pole with both hands and "cast it" up and out toward Heaven*
then trust Him and wait!"	*Clasp hands behind head and lean back, relaxed.*

Week #9 - Romans 8:26-27

WORDS	ACTIONS
"Romans chapter 8:26 and 27	*Slow, exaggerated walk (like you are "roamin'") on the beat*
I will pray with the Holy Spirit!	*Stand still and clasp hands in prayer*
The Holy Spirit will help me when I PR-AY	*With exaggerated shoulder movement—like you are coming under a burden, bring fists to belly then forward in a push*
The Holy Spirit knows just what to say!"	*Tap temple with right hand then point out from lips*

Week #10 - Romans 12:21

WORDS	ACTIONS
"Don't be overcome with evil	*Get pushed back by an invisible wave of evil*
But overcome evil with good!!	*Resolutely push invisible wave away*
Romans 12:21 uh-huh, uh-huh; Romans 12:21 uh-huh"	*Slow, exaggerated walk (like you are "roamin'") on the beat*

Week #11 - Psalms 42

WORDS	ACTIONS
"I speak to the sadness in my heart—	*Hands cupped on either side of mouth and look toward heart*
Hey, HEART! You believe!"	*Hands still cupped, shout toward heart*
I'll read some verses from Psalm 42 and	*With right hand, flip through pages of open Bible lying on left palm*
I— WILL— SING!"	*Resolutely stomp one foot* *Left hand on heart* *Right arm up and out dramatically*

Seeker's SECRET PLACE

Week #1: "The Secret Place"

MEMORY VERSES:
Psalms 91:1-2; Matthew 6:6
(Hugga Wugga™ Paraphrase)

"Kids who live in the SECRET PLACE
of the Most High (Most High)
Have a place of rest in the Shadow of the King
Psalms 91:1 and 2—God has a special home for you!
In the SECRET PLACE....In the SECRET PLACE..."

"Shhh!
Go into the SECRET PLACE
And shut the door!
Your heavenly Father hears your prayer
He WILL reward!
Matthew 6:6—Say it till it STICKS!"

Secret Sources of Power Quotes

Page 8 - From *Secret Sources of Power*
We tend to be more "problem conscious" than "power conscious." Perhaps this is why Jesus instructed His disciples on one occasion to come aside or come apart for a while. If you don't "come apart for a little while," then you might "fall apart for a long while." Jesus set the example for us by taking time to "unload" in the presence of His Father.

Page 16 - From *Secret Sources of Power*
Balanced priorities are essential. Some of us tend to become consumed with the work of God while actually neglecting our *relationship* with Him. We get so busy doing the things of God that we sacrifice our walk with God. No one was more dedicated to do the will of God than His Son Jesus. Yet, even though the whole world was lost in darkness, the Bible tells us that Jesus "came apart to rest" or went away from the crowds to be alone for a time. We need to follow His example, especially when a problem or situation threatens to consume our lives.

Page 12 - From *Secret Sources of Power*
Get with God, rest in the Father, worship Jesus, and walk in the Spirit.

WEEK #1: "The Secret Place!"

Leader's "PRAYERparation"

Please take time to thoroughly read this lesson, as well as the front pages of this curriculum, well in advance of your teaching time.

The Secret Place

There is a place we can run to when we are worried or afraid. It is a safe place where we are always welcome, and the door is never locked. Do you know where this place is? Do the children in your church know where it is? It is the Secret Place of the Most High. **Not only should we know where it is and how to get there, we need to LIVE in the Secret Place!**

Foundational Scriptures for This Lesson. *Please Read Them...*

Psalms 91:2-16 - *The Secret Place is a great place to stay!*
Psalms 32:7 - *The Lord is my Hiding Place.*
Acts 17:28 - *In Him I will live and move and have my very being.*
Mark 1:35 - *Jesus went to a solitary place to pray.*
Mark 6:31-32 - *Jesus and the disciples went together to a solitary place.*
Matthew 11:28-29 - *Come unto Me and I will give you rest; learn from Me.*
Psalms 32:7; 59:16; 62:8 - *Psalms written by David that will be read today.*

Today's Memory Verse:
Psalms 91:1-2 - Live in the Secret Place;
Matthew 6:6 - Go into the Secret Place and shut the door!

Order of Activities (Suggested)

 10 min   Welcome
Songs: "In the Secret Place";
"My Hiding Place"

 10 min   Memory Verse
(with KINGDOM RUNNER)

 15 min   Creative Illustration
"David's Secret Place"

 25 min   Secret Place Time
Songs: "In the Secret Place";
"My Hiding Place"

 30 min   Small Group Time
Making Adventure Ships

To maximize the effectiveness of this lesson, here is a **SUGGESTED LIST** of materials:

- Flashlights
- Adventure Ship Materials
- DAVID costume
- KINGDOM RUNNER costume
- Paper and pencils if you are writing letters.
- **Basics** - Overhead projector, Transparencies, CD Player, Name tags, Bibles, Small Group Pages, Secret Place Doorknob Verse

WEEK #1: "The Secret Place"

Leader & Small Group Leaders
PRAY FOR THE CHILDREN before they come into the room today, .

This prayer is based on Psalms 91:1-2 *(NKJV)* and Mark 6:31 *(God Chasers Extreme New Testament)*:

"King Jesus, we want to dwell in the Secret Place of the Most High. We want to abide under the shadow of the Almighty. Lord, You are our refuge and our fortress; our God, in You we will trust.

Today, Lord, we hear the words that You said to Your disciples, and we apply them to our lives: "Let us go away to a quiet place to be alone. We can relax a little." We want that. We want to learn to go to a quiet place and be alone with You. We want to really know what it means to relax and experience Your peace.

Bless the children of our church today. Help them learn to spend time with You in the Secret Place of Your presence. Amen."

**Welcome
10 minutes**

 LEADER (After welcoming the children): Today we are beginning a new curriculum called "Seeker's Secret Place." **God has a very special place for His children to go while they chase Him. Actually, He wants His children to LIVE there!**

 SONGS: "In the Secret Place"; "My Hiding Place"

(Suggestion: Use flashlights—one in each hand—to lead the children in simple choreography during either or both songs. Give flashlights out to as many children as possible.)

LEADER: In a few weeks, we will begin a story called, *In Search of Wanderer*. Most of you have heard stories about Seeker, right? Well, in the next story, Seeker and his sister, Moira, spend time together in the SECRET PLACE and go on a very wonderful adventure. But we don't have to wait until we hear the story—we can learn about the SECRET PLACE today! And **we won't just learn ABOUT the SECRET PLACE, we will EXPERIENCE it!**

Let's begin by reading from the King's Great Book, the Bible—and see what it says about the SECRET PLACE.

Have a child read Psalms 91:1-2 (NKJV):

He who dwells in the secret place of the Most High shall abide under the shadow of the Almighty. I will say of the Lord, "He is my refuge and my fortress; my God, in Him I will trust."

Have a child read Matthew 6:6 (NKJV):

But you, when you pray, go into your room, and when you have shut your door, pray to your Father who is in the secret place; and your Father who sees in secret will reward you openly.

Memory Verse
10 minutes

KINGDOM RUNNER comes running in, wearing work-out clothing. He runs around the room, then comes to the front and motions for the children to stand and begin running on the spot.

KINGDOM RUNNER: "Hello, Young God Chasers! How is your chase going? Are you running toward King Jesus with all your heart?! While you are chasing God, you get strength from His presence…strength from the SECRET PLACE. It's an amazing place where you can live and rest and run—all at the same time!"

Teach the Hugga-Wugga™ Paraphrase *(Hear the rhythm on the CD)*

Memory Verse #1
"Kids who live in the SECRET PLACE of the Most High (Most High)
Have a place of rest in the Shadow of the King
Psalms 91:1 and 2—God has a special home for you!
In the SECRET PLACE….In the SECRET PLACE…"

Memory Verse #2
"Shhh!
Go into the SECRET PLACE
And shut the door!
Your heavenly Father hears your prayer
He WILL reward!
Matthew 6:6—Say it till it STICKS!"

Memory Verse #1

WORDS	ACTIONS
"Kids who live in	*Hold up left forefinger*
the SECRET PLACE	*Right forefinger to lips and whisper*
of the Most High	*Point right forefinger up to Heaven*
(Most High)	*Right forefinger down then up again*
Have a place of rest in the Shadow of the King	*Bring right hand down to cover left forefinger and pull it gently to heart*
Psalm 91: 1	*Poke left forefinger up from behind right hand*
and 2	*Hold out two fingers of right hand*
God has a special home for you!	*Look down at right hand still over left forefinger at your heart*
In the SECRET PLACE….In the SECRET PLACE…"	*Keep hands the same and rock gently back and forth to the beat.*

© 2003 Dian Layton

Memory Verse #2

Memory Verse #2

WORDS	ACTIONS
"Shhh!	*Right forefinger to lips*
Go into the SECRET PLACE	
And shut the door!	
Your heavenly Father hears your prayer	
He WILL reward!	
Matthew 6:6—	*Whisper and pat legs to the beat*
Say it till it STICKS!"	*Hands get "stuck" on legs until you finally pull them off abruptly*

Creative Illustration 15 minutes

"David's Secret Place"

This is a "Kids In Ministry Opportunity!"

DAVID is dressed like a shepherd boy. He has a slingshot hanging from his back pocket.

DAVID   Hi kids! I'm David! I wanted to come and tell you about my Secret Place. My SECRET PLACE is not an actual place; it's wherever I am—because God lives in my heart so I am continually in His presence! All I need to do is whisper His name, or even just think about Him—and there I am, in the SECRET PLACE!

One thing I REALLY like to do when I'm spending time with God is to sing to Him. I make up songs all the time—just telling Him how I'm feeling and how much I love and trust Him.

LEADER   Excuse me, David—you might like to see this!

(LEADER shows DAVID the Book of Psalms in the Bible. DAVID flips through excitedly.)

DAVID   Where did you get this? Some of these look like what I've been singing to the Lord!

LEADER   Actually, many of the Psalms were written by you, David! Now they are in print—right here in the Bible!

(DAVID excitedly reads Psalms 32:7 and 62:8 aloud. Put Overhead Transparency Week One up and encourage the children to read along with David—very enthusiastically!)

Creative Illustration Cont.
"David's SECRET PLACE"

DAVID	Look right here. It says, "A Psalm of David!" "You are my hiding place; You will protect me from trouble and surround me with songs of deliverance" *(Psalms 32:7 NIV)*.
	"But I will sing of Your strength, in the morning I will sing of Your love; for You are my fortress, my refuge in times of trouble" *(Psalms 59:16 NIV)*. "A Psalm of David!"
	Wow. I knew that God was with me. I could feel Him so close when I sang. It was HIM who GAVE me the words to sing...
LEADER	And now, they are written down for all of God's people to sing, too! You can have that Bible, David.
DAVID	Thank you very much! *(He exits, reading aloud.)*
	"Everyone! Trust in the Lord at all times. Pour out your hearts to Him, because God is your refuge. He is your Hiding Place" *(From Psalms 62:8)*.

SECRET PLACE Time
25 minutes

LEADER *(After thanking DAVID)*: **The SECRET PLACE is whenever you are in God's presence.** All you need to do is think about Jesus—just whisper His name—and there you are! It is also a good idea to have a special place where you meet with Jesus. It can be beside your bed, or in a spare room in your house, or maybe you are fortunate enough to have a fort or playhouse. **It is important to have a special place where you can go and really be alone with Jesus without distractions.**

Let's find a SECRET PLACE right now! Find a place where you can concentrate on Jesus without distractions. You can sit in your chair, or kneel beside it. You can go to a corner of the room, or come and kneel up front. It would be best not to be beside your friends; they might start talking to you. This is a special time when we just want to listen to God's voice. We want to go into the SECRET PLACE and spend time with King Jesus.

We will sing the two songs we learned earlier today *(this time without flashlights)*. You can sing along, or just listen. **Really think about what the words mean...**

♫♫ SONGS: "In the Secret Place"; "My Hiding Place"

There is plenty of time in today's lesson, so enjoy this opportunity to be in the SECRET PLACE of worship! Encourage the children to find that place of rest...and to LET the King be their SECRET PLACE, their Hiding Place.

SUGGESTION: Go to Small Groups before the SECRET PLACE Time. Have the children make their Adventure Ships and then, during SECRET PLACE Time, have the children each write a letter to the King and put it in the letter box on their ship.

© 2003 Dian Layton

Small Group Time

Craft Time

Make the Adventure Ships. See the Front Pages for instructions.

**Look up these verses and discuss
what they mean in the lives of the children this week.**

TODAY'S MEMORY VERSE: Psalms 91:1-2 - *Live in the SECRET PLACE;*
Matthew 6:6 - *Go into the SECRET PLACE.*

Psalms 91:2-16 - *The SECRET PLACE is a great place to stay!*
Acts 17:28 - *In Him I will live and move and have my very being.*
Mark 1:35 - *Jesus went to a solitary place to pray.*
Mark 6:31-32 - *Jesus and the disciples went together to a solitary place.*
Matthew 11:28 - *Come unto Me and I will give you rest; learn from Me.*
Psalms 32:7; 59:16; 62:8 - *Psalms written by David that he read today.*

TALK ABOUT IT TIME

Discuss the following points from today's story:

- What is the SECRET PLACE? *(A quiet place to meet with Jesus)*

- How do you get there? *(Just think about Jesus, and there you are!)*

- Why is it important for us to spend time in the SECRET PLACE? *(To find rest and strength; to learn more about/from Jesus)*

- Do you have a special place where you go and talk to King Jesus?

SOMEONE IN THE BIBLE WHO WENT TO THE SECRET PLACE

Mark 6:31-32 - Jesus and His disciples

TOGETHER IN THE SECRET PLACE

(Not many adult prayers, please—let the children pray!)
Ask God to help you spend time with Him every day in the SECRET PLACE. Go there together right now and pray for prayer requests.

DOOR HANGER

Duplicate for the children to cut out and take home. Encourage them to hang up this week's door hanger on their bedroom doorknob when they are spending time with King Jesus in the SECRET PLACE.

Shh! I'm with King Jesus in the SECRET PLACE

MEMORY VERSES:
Psalms 91:1-2;
Matthew 6:6
(Hugga Wugga™ Paraphrase)

"Kids who live in the SECRET PLACE
of the Most High (Most High)
Have a place of rest in the Shadow of the King
Psalms 91:1 and 2—
God has a special home for you!
In the SECRET PLACE....In the SECRET PLACE..."

"Shhh!
Go into the SECRET PLACE
And shut the door!
Your heavenly Father hears your prayer
He WILL reward!
Matthew 6:6—Say it till it STICKS!"

(From Psalms 32:7 and Psalms 59:16 NIV)

"A Psalm of David!"

**"Lord, You are my hiding place;
you will protect me from trouble
and surround me with songs
of deliverance."**

**"But I will sing of Your strength,
in the morning I will sing of Your
love; for You are my fortress,
my refuge in times of trouble."**

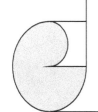 MercyPlace Ministries 9

Seeker's SECRET PLACE

Week #2:
"What Is a 'Burden'?"

MEMORY VERSE:
Matthew 11:28
(Hugga Wugga™ Paraphrase)

"Matthew 11:28—see—
Jesus said, 'Come to ME
With your heavy burdens!
And I will give you rest…Ahh…
And I will give you rest…Ahhhhh…
And I—will give—you—rest…Ahhhhhhhh…'"

Secret Sources of Power Quotes

Page 3 - From *Secret Sources of Power*
I have to wonder if some of us are trying to run our race in Christ while carrying overstuffed suitcases. Even worse, some of us are staggering down the course with a top-heavy stack of baggage so high we can't even see where we are going!

Pages 17-18 - From *Secret Sources of Power*
Are there weights in your life—things you've taken upon yourself—that are not the burden of the Lord? He wants you to lay them aside in exchange for power to run the race! Unnecessary weights will weary your mind and turn you into a zombie in the spiritual world.

God's Word says you can take care of that by unloading or flinging off that weight. If it's a sin, repent of it. If it is a weight or care you have brought on yourself, lay it aside.

Page 6 - From *Secret Sources of Power*
The redemptive blood of Jesus Christ cleanses us from all sin. Even though we want to lay aside every weight, we sometimes fail to comprehend God's power to forget. In other words, we carry the effects of sin with us when technically, they are no longer ours to bear. Once we cast them into the "sea of forgetfulness," they are only as effective in our lives as we allow them to be. We must accept God's full forgiveness and lay aside our sins and failures forever.

WEEK #2: "What Is a 'Burden'?"

Leader's "PRAYERparation"
Please take time to thoroughly read this lesson, as well as the front pages of this curriculum, well in advance of your teaching time.

What Is a Burden?

Most of the children in your church have probably asked Jesus to come into their hearts, and they understand what it means to have their sins forgiven...but they may not understand that repentance and forgiveness are parts of an ongoing, daily, continual lifestyle for Christians! When we sin, we need to just ask Jesus to forgive us and keep going, keep chasing Him. **Too many Christians are burdened with the weight of pain, shame, and guilt because they don't understand the power of Jesus' forgiveness.** Today's lesson gives each child the opportunity to ask Jesus to forgive their sins—for the first time, or as a recommitment to Him.

Foundational Scriptures for This Lesson. *Please Read Them...*

Acts 13:38-39 - *Forgiveness of sins and freedom from guilt!*
1 John 1:7-9 - *Confess your sins and continually be cleansed from sin.*

Verses from the SPIRIT-MAN booklets:
• Romans 6 verse 23—*Life without Jesus is DARK indeed.*
• Matthew 26:28...see—*Jesus died and shed His blood for you and me.*
• Isaiah chapter 1 verse 18—*Dark hearts made brand new and clean!*
• First John 5 verse 13—*You can KNOW you have life eternally.*
• First Peter 2 and verse 2—*Now we've got some growing to do!*

Today's Memory Verse:
Matthew 11:28 - *Come unto Me, all who are weary
and carry heavy burdens.*

Order of Activities (Suggested)

15 min		**Creative Illustration** **Puppet Show:** "WHYatt & WHATson" **Cheer:** "Unloading" with CANDY RAPPERS
10 min		**Memory Verse** (with KINGDOM RUNNER) **Songs:** "My Hiding Place"; "In the Secret Place"; "More, More, More"
15 min		**Creative Illustration** "Heavy Burdens" pantomime
25 min		**Secret Place Time**
25 min		**Small Group Time** Making Adventure Ships

To maximize the effectiveness of this lesson, here is a
SUGGESTED LIST of materials:

• WHYatt and WHATson puppets
• KINGDOM RUNNER costume
• CANDY RAPPERS costume
• "Heavy Burdens" pantomime costumes and props
• SPIRIT-MAN booklets
• **Basics** - Overhead projector, Transparencies, CD Player, Name tags, Bibles, Small Group Pages, SECRET PLACE Doorknob Verse

  © 2003 Dian Layton

WEEK #2: "What Is a 'Burden'?"

Leader & Small Group Leaders
PRAY FOR THE CHILDREN *before they come into the room today*, .

This prayer is based on Matthew 11:28-30 *(God Chasers Extreme New Testament)*:

"King Jesus, thank You so much that You have invited us to come to You when we are tired and have heavy loads and burdens. Thank You for Your promise to give us rest. Today we want to learn from You because You are gentle and humble in heart. You promised that the duty You give is easy. The load You put upon us is not heavy.

As we teach the principle of coming to You, help us to experience it in our own lives. Help us not to be weighed down with cares and worries, or the pain, shame, and guilt of sin—but to really know for ourselves the power of unloading our heavy burdens on You! Amen."

Creative Illustration 15 minutes

Puppet Show: "WHYatt & WHATson"

This is a "Kids In Ministry Opportunity!"

Have two puppets, each wearing a name tag with their names printed in large bold letters: "WHYatt" and "WHATson." Use a puppet theater or have the puppets behind a skirted table. WHATson carries a dictionary and speaks with a British accent. It would be fun to have him wear spectacles and a Sherlock Holmes hat. WHYatt is a typical young child who constantly asks "WHY?"

LEADER *(After welcoming the children)*: In his book, *Secret Sources of Power*, Tommy Tenney talks about one very important source of power in our lives: unloading our burdens.

WHATson	*(Suddenly poking up from puppet stage)* WHAT, may I ask, is a "burden"?
LEADER	Hello! Who are you?
WHATson	*(Points to name tag)* WHATson here! I am named that because my very most favorite thing to do is to ask the question, "WHAT"! So please, sir, tell me WHAT is a "burden"?
LEADER	A burden is something you carry…
WHATson	Like a suitcase?
LEADER	Well, yes, but not really…
WHATson	*(Echoes in surprise)* Yes, but not really? A rather vague answer, don't you think?!
LEADER	Well, a burden is like a suitcase—a suitcase you carry INSIDE.

Creative Illustration cont.
"WHYatt & WHATson"

WHATson	*(Echoes in surprise)* A suitcase you carry INSIDE?! Well, I just happen to have my handy-dandy dictionary with me! It is the best way I have found to learn more about WHAT I want to know! And I want to know exactly WHAT a burden is! *(Flips through pages...)* Blessed...boxing...brother... Ah, here it is! *(Clears throat dramatically)* Burden: "something that is carried or endured with difficulty—like pain, shame, or guilt." *(Repeats the words thoughtfully)* Something carried or endured with difficulty—like pain, shame, or guilt... Goodness, gracious! Those are some HEAVY words to talk to young children about! A burden indeed!
WHYatt	*(Suddenly poking up from puppet theater)* So WHY are you teaching little kids about heavy burdens, anyway?
LEADER	Oh! Who are you?
WHYatt	*(Points to name tag)* My name is WHYatt! And my favorite thing to do is ask the question, "WHY"! So—WHY are you teaching little kids about big heavy burdens?
LEADER	Because they need to know!
WHYatt	WHY?
LEADER	They need to know, so they won't carry them!
WHATson	Carry WHAT?
LEADER	Their heavy burdens! Children need to learn that they do not have to carry things like pain, shame, or guilt. Children need to know what King Jesus did for them! They need to know they do not have to carry the burden of SIN!

WHATson and WHYatt look at each other in silence. After a moment's pause they both nod in agreement.

WHATson	WHAT you are doing is a jolly good idea!
WHYatt	WHY, Yes! Kids need to know WHY they don't have to carry around the weight of sin—with all its pain, shame, or guiltiness!

WHYatt and WHATson exit while WHYatt speaks. LEADER smiles and waves goodbye to them.

LEADER	Well, there you have it! We are learning about WHAT burdens are and WHY we don't need to carry them! We want to be filled with God's power! How can we be filled with His power if we are already full of SIN, pain, shame, and guiltiness?

CANDY RAPPERS *(Enter running)*

CHEER: "Unloading"

© 2003 Dian Layton

Memory Verse
10 minutes

KINGDOM RUNNER comes running in, wearing workout clothing. He runs around the room, then comes to the front and motions for the children to stand and begin running on the spot.

KINGDOM RUNNER: "Hello, Young God Chasers! How is your chase going? Are you running toward King Jesus with all your heart?! Perhaps there are children here today who are chasing God, but you are feeling weary. The Great Book says: "You are tired and have heavy loads. If all of you will come to Me, I will give you rest." *(Matthew 11:28 GCENT)*

Teach the Hugga-Wugga™ paraphrase *(Hear the rhythm on the CD)*

"Matthew 11:28—see—
Jesus said, 'Come to ME
With your heavy burdens!
And I will give you rest…Ahh…
And I will give you rest…Ahhhhh…
And I—will give—you—rest…Ahhhhhhhh…'"

WORDS

"Matthew 11:28—see—

Jesus said, 'Come to ME

With your heavy burdens!

And I will give you rest…Ahh…

And I will give you rest…Ahhhhh…

And I—will give—you—rest…Ahhhhhhhh…'"

ACTIONS

Hold both hands out to the side with palms upturned, chest height

Keep hands the same; wave fingers toward chest

Pull fists to heart and be weighed down with heavy burdens that pull you to the floor in a squatting position

Get up gradually, pulling hands apart as the weight is lifted until at the end both hands are raised, totally free!

REMEMBER…..
Continue to review memory verses from previous lessons.

🎵 **SONGS**: **"My Hiding Place"**; **"In the Secret Place"**; **"More, More, More"**

"Heavy Burdens" pantomime

Creative Illustration 15 minutes

This is a "Kids In Ministry Opportunity!"

CHARACTERS: MIME, JESUS, and a GOD CHASER with a Bible; TWO TALL CHILDREN. PROPS: A suitcase and stones. *(Suggestion: the stones can be real, or paper-mache, or newspaper that has been crumpled up, formed into balls, and spray-painted gray.)* You will need a total of 8 stones labeled: "SIN," "PAIN," "SHAME," "GUILT," "TROUBLES," "FEARS," "WORRIES," and "DISAPPOINTMENT," a large blue sheet labeled "SEA OF FORGETFUL-NESS" held up like a screen by the TWO TALL CHILDREN.

Play the sound trax of "You Are My Hiding Place" in the background.

NARRATION	PANTOMIME
The child was carefree and happy Laughing, and singing all day Not a care nor a worry to think of Nothing to do but play.	**MIME** *dances around happily in a small area, stopping to smell flowers and to pet a bird perched on his/her hand…*
Time passed and soon the child realized A whole world was waiting for him And the child began exploring With great enthusiasm!	**MIME** *walks along the path, excitedly looking around and exploring the world that is beginning to open up…*
But as the child walked along life's pathway He picked up burdens and cares Never understanding They were not his to bear…	**MIME** *bends to pick up stones labeled "SIN" and "GUILT."* **JESUS** *enters and stands in the background.*
Someone the child loved and trusted Hurt him—again and again…and again… The child grew worried and frightened And his heart filled up with pain.	**JESUS** *reaches out toward the child but the child doesn't see Him.* **MIME** *puts both arms up protectively while backing away to avoid being hit. Then picks up heavy stones labeled "PAIN" and "SHAME" and carries them.*
Then so-called friends spoke cruel words And said things that were not true The child carried disappointment Because he didn't know what else to do.	**JESUS** *reaches out again toward the child but the child doesn't see Him.* **MIME** *puts fingers in his ears and shakes his head back and forth, trying to shut out the words.* **MIME** *finds the suitcase, where he/she puts the stones; then picks up "WORRIES" and "FEAR" and adds them to the suitcase.*
The weeks, months, and years continued As the child journeyed along Gathering more heavy burdens From everything that went wrong.	**JESUS** *continues to reach out.* **MIME** *stops along path to add another heavy stone labeled "DISAPPOINTMENT" and walks on…*

© 2003 Dian Layton

Creative Illustration cont.
"Heavy Burdens" pantomime

The child did not realize
That he was not alone
Someone walked beside him
There upon life's road

*JESUS walks beside the **MIME**, who is struggling with the heavy weight of the suitcase.*
***GOD CHASER** enters happily and hugs JESUS.*
***JESUS** points to the MIME and the **GOD CHASER** nods.*

But one day he heard the good news
And happily believed
His eyes and ears were open
Jesus said, "Child, come to Me."

***GOD CHASER** goes to the MIME and shows him/her places in the Bible.*
***MIME** looks hopeful, then gradually understands.*
***GOD CHASER** leads MIME over to JESUS. **MIME** lays down the suitcase and hugs JESUS. **GOD CHASER** watches happily then exits.*

"Come to Me with your heavy burdens!"
That is what Jesus said.
"Come to Me with your heavy burdens!
And I will give you rest."

***MIME** picks up the suitcase and turns to take JESUS' hand.*
***JESUS** shakes his head, sits down, and motions for the MIME join Him. **MIME** gratefully sets down the suitcase and leans against JESUS saying, "Ahhh."*
*After a few moments, **JESUS** "asks permission" to open the suitcase.*

TWO TALL CHILDREN bring in the "SEA OF FORGETFULNESS"
and hold it taut; then turn it and hold like a sort of hammock.

***JESUS** opens the suitcase very tenderly. **MIME** winces with pain. One by one, the **MIME** gives his/her burdens to Jesus. It is a healing process—giving the burden to JESUS. He takes it and throws it into the SEA; then places a hand on MIME'S heart to heal the hurt.*
*Soon the suitcase is empty. **MIME** is obviously relieved and leans peacefully against JESUS again.*

TWO TALL CHILDREN carry the SEA with all the burdens, as well as the suitcase, away.

The child was again carefree and happy
Laughing and singing all day
Not a care nor a worry to think of
Because JESUS had taken every burden away!
Ahhh…

***JESUS** helps **MIME** stand up and they dance away.*

**Secret Place
Time
25 minutes**

LEADER *(Lead in applause.)*: I know there are **some of you here who have been carrying heavy burdens**…like a heavy suitcase inside…and today, I want to be like that God Chaser in the skit. I want to help you understand how Jesus took your burdens all away so you don't have to carry them! He took your sin, your pain, shame, and guiltiness.

Some people ask Jesus to forgive their sins when they first receive Him into their heart…then, after that, whenever they sin, they don't repent. They just feel guilty and try and try and try to do better. Listen, you can't get rid of sin by trying to do better! The Bible tells us the only way to get rid of SIN is to repent. Repentance is simply turning **AWAY from SIN** and turning **TOWARD GOD.**

Something else that people do is to keep asking Jesus to come into their heart over and over again. That's like their SPIRIT-MAN getting born-again again and again! Boys and girls, when you ask Jesus to come into your heart, HE DOES! And then, He wants to HELP you do what is right! **When you sin, don't go around feeling guilty—just repent and keep on living for Jesus!**

Please stand up very quietly, not looking around. We are in the SECRET PLACE. If you have **never ever asked Jesus to forgive your sins** and come into your heart—you can right now. Or, if you have asked Jesus into your heart but today **you want to repent…you want to ask His forgiveness** for things you've been doing wrong—you can right now. In fact, before we pray, let's all listen for His voice. **Lord, we ask You right now to show us areas of sin in our lives** that we need to repent from…*(Wait and listen for His voice before proceeding.)*

Please close your eyes, put your hands on your heart, and pray after me…

"King Jesus, *(children echo)* You see inside my heart. *(children echo)* You know how I feel inside. *(children echo)* Your Word says to come to You *(children echo)* with my heavy burdens. *(children echo)* So Lord, here I am. *(children echo)* I give You my heavy burdens. *(children echo)* I give You all my sin, *(children echo)* my pain, shame, and guiltiness. *(children echo)* I ask You, King Jesus, to forgive me. *(children echo)* I repent from my sin. *(children echo)* I turn to You and give you all my heavy burdens. *(children echo)* I give you all my sin. Thank You, JESUS! *(children echo)* Thank You that it is now in the Sea of Forgetfulness! *(children echo)* And I am free from every heavy burden! *(children echo)* Ahhh… *(children echo)*"

"In the Secret Place" and "You Are My Hiding Place" softly in background.

Invite the children to come and kneel at the front if they would like extra prayer. Have Small Group Leaders and other children come and pray with them. Be sensitive to the Lord and to the children. After an appropriate amount of time, quietly break into Small Groups while allowing those children who are still praying to continue to do so.

Small Group Time

Small Group
25 minutes

Look up these verses and discuss what they mean in the lives of the children this week.

TODAY'S MEMORY VERSE: Matthew 11:28 - Come unto Me, all who are weary and carry heavy burdens.

Acts 13:38-39 - Forgiveness of sins and freedom from guilt!
1 John 1:7-9 - Confess your sins and continually be cleansed from sin.

TALK ABOUT IT TIME
Discuss the following points from today's story:

- **What did you learn from the puppet show?** *(WHAT a burden is and WHY we shouldn't carry them!)*

- **What is a burden?** *(Something we carry inside—like sin, pain, shame, and guiltiness.)*

- **Why shouldn't we carry burdens?** *(They are too heavy; JESUS wants to carry them for us.)*

- **Did you give your heavy burdens to JESUS today? How did that feel?**

SPIRIT-MAN BOOKLETS
Today we have a gift for each one of you. *(Hand out SPIRIT-MAN booklets.)* At the back of the booklet is a page with a prayer and a place to put your name and today's date if you prayed to receive Jesus as your Savior, or if you repented of your sin and made a re-commitment to Him. You can also use the booklet as a gift for someone else who doesn't know Jesus. *(Go through the booklet as a group, taking time to look up the Scriptures.)*

SOMEONE IN THE BIBLE WHO GAVE THEIR BURDEN OF SIN TO THE LORD
Luke 7:47 - The sinful woman who came to Jesus

TOGETHER IN THE SECRET PLACE
Thank King Jesus for taking your sin away. Pray for people you know who are not yet Christians and who need to hear the message in the SPIRIT-MAN booklet.

DOOR HANGER

Duplicate for the children to cut out and take home. Encourage them to hang up this week's door hanger on their bedroom doorknob when they are spending time with King Jesus in the SECRET PLACE.

Shh! I'm with King Jesus in the Secret Place

MEMORY VERSE:
Matthew 11:28
(Hugga Wugga™ Paraphrase)

"Matthew 11:28—see—
Jesus said, 'Come to ME
With your heavy burdens!
And I will give you rest…Ahh…
And I will give you rest…Ahhhhh…
And I—will give—you—rest…Ahhhhhhhh…'

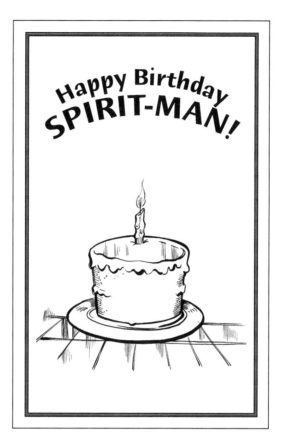

SPIRIT-MAN BOOKLETS

The SPIRIT-MAN Booklets provided in this curriculum will be a valuable tool. Photocopy the pages front and back in order and staple them together. Keep plenty on hand to use as needed.

Happy Birthday SPIRIT-MAN!

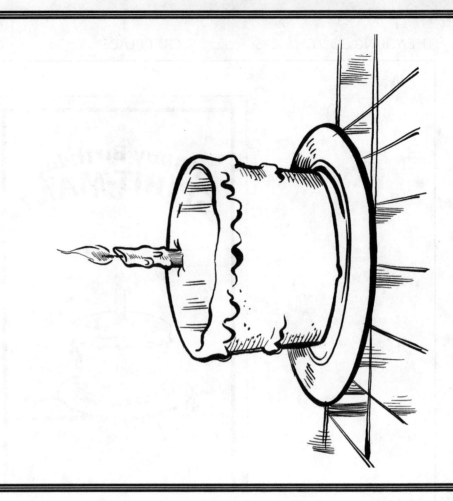

First Peter 2 and verse 2
Now we've got some growing to do!

Your SPIRIT-MAN wants to grow up to be big and strong and healthy! Here are some ways to help your SPIRIT-MAN grow.

GOD'S WORD, THE BIBLE—Whenever you read the Bible, listen to the Bible, or especially, MEMORIZE the Bible, you are feeding your SPIRIT-MAN! *(See 1 Peter 2:2)*

PRAYER and WORSHIP—Whenever you spend time with Jesus, your SPIRIT-MAN gets stronger! *(See Jude 20 and 2 Corinthians 3:18)*

OTHER CHRISTIANS—When you are "born again" you are born into God's family, and you are one of His children! Being with your brothers and sisters in the Lord is a source of nourishment and strength for SPIRIT-MAN! *(See Hebrew 10:25 and Matthew 18:20)*

FEED YOUR SPIRIT-MAN!

G od made the world. He made the sun, moon, stars, oceans, rivers, mountains, and trees. The first people God made to live on the earth were Adam and Eve. They lived in a beautiful garden called "Eden."

Adam and Eve could go where they wanted, do what they wanted, eat what they wanted...except for one thing. There was one rule. Wouldn't it be nice if you only had ONE RULE to remember?!

Here is how to receive Jesus into your heart and be born again...

Giving your life to Jesus means giving your life to Jesus! It's not yours any more. It belongs to Him—and that makes Him the Lord, the BOSS of your life. Do you REALLY want to do that?

If you have NEVER asked Jesus into your heart, OR if you just aren't SURE if you are a Christian, and you want to make sure today, OR, if you feel like you want to make a new commitment to live for Jesus and not for yourself, here is a prayer you can pray.

Lord Jesus, thank You so much for taking my punishment. Thank You for dying on the cross for my sins. Lord Jesus, please forgive me for all my sin. Forgive me for all the ways I have served myself; for all the ways I have gone my own way instead of Your way.

Today I ask You, Jesus, to come into my heart. Make me born again. Make my SPIRIT-MAN come alive. Thank You, Jesus, that from now on my life is Yours. I am a Christian. Help me to live for You—every day—for the rest of my life. Amen!

RECORD OF MY DECSION

Today, _____ (date) _____ (name)

☐ Received Jesus' gift of eternal life and was BORN AGAIN!

☐ Made a new commitment to live for Jesus everyday!

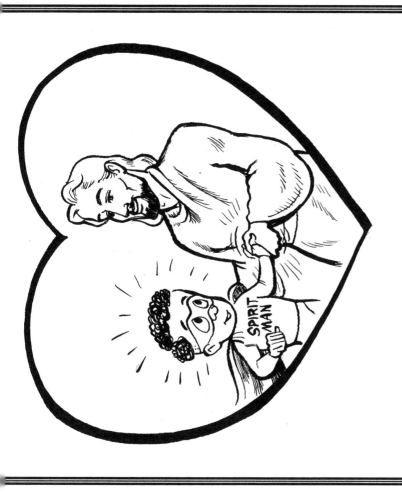

First John 5 verse 13
You can KNOW you have life eternally.

Some people think that they can get to Heaven by being kind and doing good things. That is not true.

There is only ONE WAY to have eternal life, and that is to receive Jesus into your heart and be born again. It is important to be kind and good, but that will not get you to Heaven. You are a sinner and you need a Savior. You could do good, kind things every day of your life, but that would not make your SPIRIT-MAN come to life.

Only Jesus can make you born again!

In the garden was a tree called the Tree of the Knowledge of Good and Evil. Of every other tree, Adam and Eve could eat all they wanted...but from THIS tree they could not eat. If they did, God told them that IN THAT DAY they would die. (*See Genesis 2:17.*)

Adam and Eve disobeyed the one and only rule. They ate the fruit from the forbidden tree. They sinned.

Did they die? God said, "In that day you will surely die." But, did they die?

Yes. The part of them that would have lived forever, their spirit, died; and their physical bodies began to die that day. The penalty, the punishment for sin, is death and separation from God.

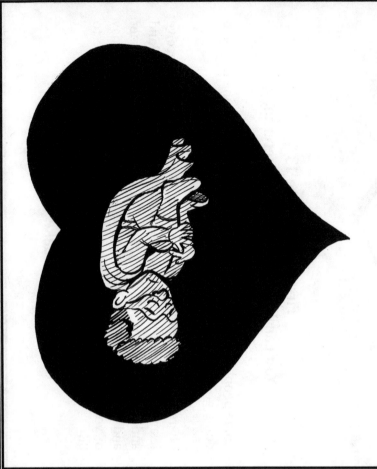

Romans 6 verse 23
Life without Jesus is DARK indeed.

The Bible tells us that ever since that time, every person has been born as a sinner. Every person is dead—spiritually. We are all sinners. Do you know what sin is? Sin means going our own way instead of God's way. It means doing what we want to do instead of what God wants us to do. And the punishment, the disciple for sin is death and separation form God.

Suppose you did something wrong and you were just about to be punished. Then a friend knocked on the door and said, "Wait! I will take that punishment! I will take the discipline instead!"

Would you like that? If your friend took your punishment, would you have to? No, you would be free! Wouldn't that be wonderful?

5

Isaiah chapter 1 verse 18
Dark hearts made brand new and clean!

And when you do that, a miracle happens! Your spirit, which was dead in trespasses and sins, comes to life! John chapter 3, verse 3 calls it being "born again." You are alive inside! The Bible says that you come out of darkness into the Kingdom of Light! (See Colossians 1:12-13.) It is your birthday!

8

Matthew 26:28...see—
Jesus died and shed His blood for you and me.

Jesus Christ, whose name is Immanuel, God WITH us, came to this world and offered His life as a punishment for our sins.

He willingly went to the cross and died...for every person.

He died for you.

He took YOUR sin upon Himself.

And all you have to do is believe that. All you have to do is receive what He did for you. All you have to do is say,

"Yes, Jesus, I believe that You died for me. I am a sinner and I need You to be my Savior. Thank You for taking the punishment for my sin. Today, I receive Your gift of LIFE!"

That is exactly what Jesus did for us.

The punishment for sin is death.

Jesus stood up and said, "Wait! I'll take their punishment! I will die in their place."

The Baby born in a manger at Christmas was no ordinary baby! He was KING JESUS—disguised as a human being.

We are all sinners. Sinners need a Savior.

Seeker's SECRET PLACE

Week #3:
"Unloading Your Burdens"

MEMORY VERSE:
Hebrews 12:1
(Hugga Wugga™ Paraphrase)

"Get rid of anything that slows you down
And don't let SIN tie you up! (Uh-uh!)
Keep on running the race ahead
That's Hebrew 12, verse 1! (Uh-HUH!)
That's Hebrew 12, verse 1! (Uh-HUH!)"

Secret Sources of Power Quotes

Pages 5-6 - From *Secret Sources of Power*

Life gets difficult when we give too much "weight" to the things we cannot change in life. The first thing we should do is make sure we aren't carrying the weight of any sin in our lives….

We all need to repent. It is the biblical way to *"lay aside every weight, and the sin which so easily ensnares us."*

Page 27 - From *Secret Sources of Power*

Are you ready and willing to unload? Don't be like some people who have such a tight claim on their problems that they wouldn't take a million dollars for them. Their conversations are peppered with possessive statements like, "*My* heart problem…" and "*My* problems with my children…" Why claim the problems? All that whining only lets the devil know you are in his neighborhood.

Even Jesus had to unload the weight of the cross temporarily. Simon carried the cross of Christ for a distance. If He couldn't reach the destination of His destiny without unloading, neither can you! He unloaded in order to reload and finish the course. Don't let present pressures postpone future destiny. There is power in proper unloading!

WEEK #3: "Unloading Your Burdens"

Leader's "PRAYERparation"

Please take time to thoroughly read this lesson, as well as the front pages of this curriculum, well in advance of your teaching time.

Unloading Your Burdens

Many people spend time in counseling sessions trying to get free of the sin, pain, shame, and guiltiness they have been carrying around for years. In this curriculum, you have the wonderful opportunity to teach children how to continually **"cast all their cares"** and **"unload their heavy burdens"** on Jesus. Our prayer is that what the children learn during the next weeks will establish a pattern of response and behavior that will last a lifetime!

Foundational Scriptures for This Lesson. *Please Read Them...*

Galatians 5:1 - *Jesus made you free from sin;*
don't get tangled up in it again!
Psalms 62:8 - *O my people, trust in Him at all times.*
Pour out your heart to Him, for God is our refuge.
1 Peter 5:7 - *Casting all your care upon Him, because He cares for you.*
1 Samuel 17:34-37 - *David was protected from the lion and the bear.*
Psalms 55:22 - *Give your burdens to the LORD, and He will take care of you.*
Romans 15:14; 2 Corinthians 7:4; Colossians 1:9; Nehemiah 8:10 -
Some things God WANTS you to be filled with.

Today's Memory Verse:
Hebrews 12:1 - *Get rid of anything that slows you down!*

Order of Activities (Suggested)

15 min **Creative Illustration**
"David's Secret Place"
Songs: "In the Secret Place";
"My Hiding Place"; "More, More, More";
"I'm Loved by God"

10 min **Memory Verse**
(with KINGDOM RUNNER)

15 min **Creative Illustration**
"SPIRIT-MAN"
Cheer: "Unloading" with CANDY RAPPERS

25 min **Secret Place Time**

25 min **Small Group Time**

To maximize the effectiveness
of this lesson, here is a
SUGGESTED LIST of materials:

- KINGDOM RUNNER costume
- DAVID costume
- SPIRIT-MAN costumes and props
- CANDY RAPPERS costume
- **Basics** - Overhead projector,
Transparencies, CD Player,
Name tags, Bibles, Small Group Pages,
Secret Place Doorknob Verse

WEEK #3: "Unloading Your Burdens"

Leader & Small Group Leaders
PRAY FOR THE CHILDREN before they come into the room today, .

This prayer is based on Hebrews 12: 1-3 *(God Chasers Extreme New Testament)*:

"King Jesus, thank you for the race that is ahead of us. Please help us to put aside anything that might slow us down. Sin can easily tie us up. Let us run with endurance the race that is ahead of us. Lord, You endured when You had to suffer shame and die on a cross. Why? Because of the happiness that lay ahead for You. You didn't mind the way You had to die. Help us to keep our eyes on You, Jesus. You are the beginning and the goal of our faith. Lord, You are the One we are chasing and pursuing. Help us to run the race and pursue You with all our hearts! Amen."

Creative Illustration 15 minutes

"David's Secret Place"

This is a "Kids In Ministry Opportunity!"

DAVID is dressed like a shepherd boy. He has a slingshot hanging from his back pocket. He also has his Bible. He enters, running and excited.

DAVID: Hi, kids! I'm David! I just HAD to come and tell you what happened! I look after my father's sheep. There I was in my SECRET PLACE, watching the sheep and singing new songs to the Lord like usual, when all of a sudden a lion came and carried off a sheep from the flock. I went after the lion, struck it, and rescued the sheep from its mouth. When the lion turned on me, I seized it by its hair, struck it and killed it. Then the same thing happened with a bear! Listen to me! I had a LOT of troubles—a LOT of heavy burdens—but the Lord who delivered me from the paw of the lion and the paw of the bear will deliver YOU from all your troubles! Trust in the Lord! Spend time with Him in the Secret Place! *(He exits, reading aloud.)*

"You are my hiding place; You will protect me from trouble and surround me with songs of deliverance" (Psalms 32:7 NIV).

🎵 **SONGS: "My Hiding Place"; "In the Secret Place"; "More, More, More"**
NEW SONG: "I'm Loved by God"

Explain the following words from the song:

Aggravate: annoy, frustrate, make angry

Intimidate: frighten, discourage, dishearten

Separate: split off, break apart

Creative Illustration cont.

 LEADER *(After welcoming the children)*: Can anyone tell me what we learned last week? What is a "burden"? *(Something heavy that we carry inside: like sin, pain, shame, and guiltiness.)*

Today's lesson is called, "Unloading Your Burdens." **Giving your burdens to King Jesus is not something you do ONCE. King Jesus wants us to ALWAYS GIVE Him our heavy burdens.** Can you tell me some reasons **WHY** He wants these? I mean—it sounds pretty strange when you stop to think about it. What if I were to come to you *(walk over to a child)* and say, "Hi, there—give me all your burdens. I really want them! PLEASE—can I have your burdens? Please?" That would seem strange, wouldn't it? **Why would King Jesus want our burdens?**

Allow response. Steer the children toward statements like "He loves us,"
"He wants to look after us," etc.

Those are all correct answers. Today I want to tell you a VERY IMPORTANT reason why God wants you to give Him all your burdens: **So you can run the race and WIN!**

Boys and girls, **each one of us is running a race**. Life is like a track spread out in front of us, and Jesus is with us as we run, and He will meet us at the finish line.

Memory Verse
10 minutes

KINGDOM RUNNER comes running in, wearing workout clothing. He runs around the room, then comes to the front and motions for the children to stand and begin running on the spot.

 KINGDOM RUNNER: "Hello, Young God Chasers! How is your chase going? Are you running toward King Jesus with all your heart?! The Great Book says that you are in a race...and every single one of you can win! It's right here in Hebrews 12 verse 1...

Read today's memory verses from the Bible:

"...We must put aside anything that might slow us down. Sin can easily tie us up. Let us run with endurance the race that is ahead of us." *(Hebrews 12:1 GCENT)*

Teach the Hugga-Wugga™ paraphrase *(Hear the rhythm on the CD)*

"Get rid of anything that slows you down
And don't let SIN tie you up! (Uh-uh!)
Keep on running the race ahead
That's Hebrew 12, verse 1! (Uh-HUH!)
That's Hebrew 12, verse 1! (Uh-HUH!)"

Memory Verse cont.

WORDS	ACTIONS
	Run on the spot
"Get rid of anything that slows you down	*Continue to run while pulling off an invisible heavy coat*
And don't let SIN	*Forearms crossed at chest; make fists*
tie you up!	*Fist rotate over fist several times*
(Uh-uh!)	*Break free!*
Keep on running the race ahead	*Run on the spot with greater determination*
That's Hebrew 12, verse 1! (Uh-HUH!)	
That's Hebrew 12, verse 1! (Uh-HUH!)"	*Stretch - touching toes left, then right*

REMEMBER.....
Continue to review memory verses from previous lessons.

Creative Illustration
15 minutes

"SPIRIT-MAN"

NOTE: The person who plays the part of SPIRIT-MAN today must be willing to stay for the whole meeting and must be willing to open his/her heart up about some area he/she struggles in so the children can really learn today's lesson principles from a practical demonstration. A blank has been provided for you to put the person's real name.

SPIRIT-MAN wears a white T-shirt with the letters: "S-P-I-R-I-T-M-A-N" across the front, a brightly colored eye mask and a shining cape. This time he has a backpack on his back. It is filled with large rocks. The largest rock is on top and it is labeled "GUILT." He is also tangled in a rope labeled "SIN."

SPIRIT-MAN enters, trying to run but he is weighed down with his heavy backpack and keeps tripping on the rope.

LEADER   Hello there, SPIRIT-MAN! Hey, you look like _____! *(Insert name of the real person who is playing the part of SPIRIT-MAN)*

Creative Illustration cont.
"SPIRIT-MAN"

SPIRIT-MAN	That's because I'm _____'s SPIRIT-MAN! *(He leans against the wall, panting.)*
LEADER	Oh! Well, you don't look too good! What is wrong with you?
SPIRIT-MAN	Uh, I'm just trying my best to chase God with all my heart. I'm trying to run the race of life! *(Runs a bit more, then stops, huffing and puffing wearily.)* But I'm not getting very far…
LEADER	Well, that rope has you all tangled up…and it looks like your backpack is too heavy. Where did the rope come from, anyway?
SPIRIT-MAN	*(Shrugs)* Well, _____ hasn't really been doing everything he knows God wants him to lately…Actually, he's been doing some things that are downright wrong! And every time he sins, the rope winds around me more!
LEADER	Hmm…the Bible talks about not being tangled up in SIN. What about the backpack? What do you have in there, anyway?
SPIRIT-MAN	Oh, just a few things from life…you know, stuff I carry around for _____. It just seems to be getting a lot heavier lately.
LEADER	Can I take a look and see what it is that you are carrying?
SPIRIT-MAN	*(Sits down gratefully.)* Sure, go ahead.
LEADER	*(Opens backpack and gasps. Then pulls out the large and OBVIOUSLY VERY HEAVY rock labeled "GUILT" and sets it down.)* Why are you carrying GUILT around?
SPIRIT-MAN	*(Shrugs)* Well, like I said, _____ hasn't really been doing everything he knows God wants him to lately. When he sins, it makes him feel guilty. And it makes ME feel worn out! Whew! I don't know how much longer I can carry this! *(Wipes his brow.)*
LEADER	You shouldn't be carrying it at all!
SPIRIT-MAN	*(Surprised)* I shouldn't?!
LEADER	No way! That's Jesus' job!
SPIRIT-MAN	What?! You want Jesus to carry that heavy thing around?

Creative Illustration cont.
"SPIRIT-MAN"

LEADER Of course! He took ALL of our GUILT when He died on the cross—He doesn't want us to still be carrying it around! And this rope—Jesus broke the power of SIN so that we don't have to be tangled up in it!

Boys and girls, let's say today's memory verse for SPIRIT-MAN! *(Review Hebrews 12:1)*

Listen, SPIRIT-MAN, I think it would be a good idea for _____ to hear today's lesson. *(Puts the rock back into the backpack.)* He needs to let Jesus break the power of SIN in his life and carry all of his guilt.

SPIRIT-MAN *(Stands, struggling under the weight.)* That's for sure! Because I really can't carry this! Thanks a lot! I sure hope _____ gets the message so I can get rid of this heavy burden and get out of this tangled rope!

SPIRIT-MAN exits, panting and struggling. _____ takes off the SPIRIT-MAN costume and comes back into the room during the CANDY RAPPER cheer.

 CANDY RAPPERS *(Enter running)*
CHEER: "Unloading"

TESTIMONY: The person who played the part of SPIRIT-MAN steps forward and asks for prayer. He says that the cheer just helped him to realize why it's been so difficult lately for him to chase God like he used to. Instead of being filled with Jesus, he has been filled with GUILT and SIN. *(Idea: Have the person share something REAL that he actually struggles with. Have a few of the children come and pray for him. This would not be a skit. It would need to be genuine.)*

 LEADER *(Speaks to the person as they finish their testimony.)* The Bible tells us the way to get rid of SIN is to repent. Repentance is simply turning away from SIN and turning toward God. Are you ready to repent from your SIN and turn with all your heart toward Jesus?

The person says that yes, he/she is ready and prays a simple prayer of repentance out loud.

 LEADER *(Leads in thankful applause to King Jesus and hugs the person.)* There! Now your SPIRIT-MAN will feel a lot better!

Secret Place Time 25 minutes

Turn the lights down low so the children will feel more comfortable. The following is a suggestion of what you can say, quietly and unobtrusively.

Boys and girls, burdens in our hearts slow us down and make it hard for us to really CHASE GOD. King Jesus wants us to UNLOAD all our cares on Him, and then He wants to give us His joy and strength to be ABLE to run the race He has set before us.

Let's all go into the SECRET PLACE and be with King Jesus.

Please, no one looking around or talking. The person beside you might be carrying some very heavy burdens, and we don't want anything to distract them from giving their burdens to King JESUS.

Everyone, **please picture JESUS standing there beside you. This is not pretending! He REALLY IS with you!** When we get to the part of the prayer where we give all our heavy burdens to JESUS, I want you to do a sort of pantomime. I want you **to pull all your burdens—your sin, pain, shame, guilt, troubles, fears, and worries—anything that is weighing you down inside and give it all up to the Lord!** Okay? Then we are going to ask King Jesus to touch your heart and **FILL it with joy and strength instead** of the heavy burdens that were there.

Please close your eyes, put your hands on your heart, and pray after me…

> "King Jesus, *(children echo)* You said to get rid of anything that slows me down, *(children echo)* and not to let SIN tie me up. *(children echo)* I want to run the race ahead with all my might! *(children echo)* So I need to get rid of all my heavy burdens, *(children echo)* and the sin that tries to tie me up. *(children echo)* King Jesus, I repent from my sin. *(children echo)* I turn to You *(children echo)* and I give You all my heavy burdens. *(children echo)* And now, I put my hand on my heart *(children echo)* and I pull out the pain, shame, and guiltiness. *(children echo)* I pull out all my troubles, fears, and worries. *(children echo)* And I give it all to You! *(children echo)* Thank You, JESUS! *(children echo)* I am free from every heavy burden! *(children echo)* I am free to run the race ahead with all my might! *(children echo)* Now I ask You, Lord, *(children echo)* to fill my heart *(children echo)* with Your joy, and peace, and strength. *(children echo)* Amen."

"In the Secret Place" and "You Are My Hiding Place" softly in background.

Invite the children to come and kneel at the front if they would like extra prayer. Have Small Group Leaders and other children come and pray with them. Be sensitive to the Lord and to the children. Watch for any children who are weeping. What they will need most is someone to just hold them and let them cry. If they want to talk, fine, but otherwise, just hold them and pray very quietly. Let God's voice be the one they hear.

After an appropriate amount of time, quietly break into Small Groups while allowing those children who are still praying to continue to do so.

© 2003 Dian Layton

Small Group Time

Look up these verses and discuss what they mean in the lives of the children this week.

TODAY'S MEMORY VERSE: Hebrews 12:1 - Get rid of anything that slows you down!

Galatians 5:1 - Jesus made you free from sin; don't get tangled up in it again!
Psalms 62:8 - O my people, trust in Him at all times. Pour out your heart to Him, for God is our refuge.
1 Peter 5:7 - Casting all your care upon Him; because He cares for you.
1 Samuel 17:34-37 - David was protected from the lion and the bear.
Psalms 55:22 - Give your burdens to the LORD, and He will take care of you.
Romans 15:14; 2 Corinthians 7:4; Colossians 1:9; Nehemiah 8:10 - Some things God WANTS you to be filled with.

TALK ABOUT IT TIME
Discuss the following points from today's story:

- **What is a burden?** *(Something we carry inside—like sin, pain, shame, and guiltiness.)*

- **Why does Jesus want to carry our burdens?** *(He wants us to be free to run the race ahead.)*

- **Do you know someone who is carrying a heavy burden and needs our prayers today?**

SOMEONE IN THE BIBLE WHO GAVE THEIR BURDEN OF SIN TO THE LORD
I Samuel 1:10-18 - Hannah

TOGETHER IN THE SECRET PLACE
(Not many adult prayers, please—let the children pray!)
Most of the children will be able to very quickly think about an adult or teenager who is carrying heavy burdens. Spend time praying for those people. Pray today's memory verse and also last week's verse:

- Pray that people will get rid of anything that slows them down, and not let SIN tie them up! Pray that they will keep on running the race ahead…
- Pray that they will go to JESUS with their heavy burdens and that He will give them rest. Ahhh!

DOOR HANGER

Duplicate for the children to cut out and take home. Encourage them to hang up this week's door hanger on their bedroom doorknob when they are spending time with King Jesus in the SECRET PLACE.

Shh! I'm with King Jesus in the Secret Place

MEMORY VERSE:
Hebrews 12:1
(Hugga Wugga™ Paraphrase)

*"Get rid of anything that slows you down
And don't let SIN tie you up! (Uh-uh!)
Keep on running the race ahead
That's Hebrew 12, verse 1! (Uh-HUH!)
That's Hebrew 12, verse 1! (Uh-HUH!)"*

Week #4:
"Choose to Forgive"

MEMORY VERSES:
Matthew 6; Ephesians 4:32
(Hugga Wugga™ Paraphrase)

"From Matthew chapter 6:
The Lord's Prayer...and beyond...
Lord, forgive my sins in exactly the same way
I choose to forgive other people."

"Be kind to one another
Tenderhearted
Forgiving one another
'Cause God's forgiven you!
Ephesians 4 verse - 32!"

Secret Sources of Power Quotes

Page 25 - From *Secret Sources of Power*

Sooner or later someone will disappoint or fail you in some way. Don't allow that hurt to become a bitter place in your heart. Let it go, lay it aside, unload it at Jesus' feet.

Pages 39-40 - From *Secret Sources of Power*

There is power in forgiveness. Do you remember Jesus' parable about the man who owed his king ten thousand talents?...

This man who had been forgiven for a multi-million-dollar debt showed no mercy to the man who owed him only 20 dollars; instead he had him thrown into jail until he could repay his debt...Jesus bluntly warned His listeners then and now: "So My heavenly Father also will do to you if each of you, from his heart, does not forgive his brother his trespasses" (Mt. 18:35).

If you have that kind of spirit, cancel it. The only money the unmerciful servant had available to loan to his victim was the money loaned to him by the king! He should have offered his debtor some of the forgiveness he had received from the king. The only forgiveness we have to give is what we receive from God. We aren't any different from the servant who owed an unpayable debt: The Lord has forgiven each of us of a "multi-million-dollar debt." Don't you think we should be quick to forgive our brother or sister of their "20-dollar debt" to us? (We can't afford to say, "No.")

Page 29 - From *Secret Sources of Power*

It is a difficult assignment for such imperfect people, but there is a secret source of power in forgiveness for those with eyes to see and a will to obey.

NOTE: It would be very helpful for you to read all of Chapters 3 and 4 in
Secret Sources of Power in preparation for this week's lesson.

WEEK #4: "Choose to Forgive"

Leader's "PRAYERparation"

Please take time to thoroughly read this lesson, as well as the front pages of this curriculum, well in advance of your teaching time.

Choose to Forgive

"I'm not your friend anymore!" "I'll never forgive you!" Statements like these are spoken far too often by children. Unforgiveness is a tremendous burden that some people carry for many years. This week's lesson will help the children realize the **importance, and the power of forgiveness**…now, and for the rest of their lives. Forgiveness is not optional.

Foundational Scriptures for This Lesson. *Please Read Them…*

Matthew 6: 9-13 - *The Lord's Prayer.*
Matthew 18:21-22 - *Forgive seventy times seven times.*
Matthew 18:22-35 - *Jesus told the parable of the unforgiving servant.*
Mark 11:25-26 - *When you stand praying, forgive.*
Matthew 6:14-15; 18:35; Mark 11:26; Luke 6:37 -
If you want God to forgive you, you MUST forgive other people.
Luke 23:34; Hebrews 12:3 - *Think about what Jesus had to suffer, and He still chose to forgive!*

Today's Memory Verse:
Matthew 6:12, 14-15 - *Forgive me AS I forgive other people;*
Ephesians 4:32 - *Be kind to one another and forgive.*

Order of Activities (Suggested)

15 min  **Welcome**
Cheer: "Unloading" with CANDY RAPPERS
Songs: "I'm Loved by God";
"More, More, More";

10 min **Memory Verse**
(with KINGDOM RUNNER)

25 min **Creative Illustration**
"The Unforgiving"

20 min **Secret Place Time**
Songs: "In the SECRET PLACE";
"My Hiding Place"

20 min **Small Group Time**

To maximize the effectiveness
of this lesson, here is a
SUGGESTED LIST of materials:

• KINGDOM RUNNER costume
• SPIRIT-MAN costumes and props
• CANDY RAPPERS costume
• "The Unforgiving Servant"
Costumes and Props
• **Basics** - Overhead projector,
Transparencies, CD Player,
Name tags, Bibles, Small Group Pages,
Secret Place Doorknob Verse

© 2003 Dian Layton

WEEK #4: "Choose to Forgive"

Leader & Small Group Leaders
PRAY FOR THE CHILDREN *before they come into the room today, .*

This prayer is based on Psalms 91:1-2 NKJV) and Mark 6:31 (God Chasers Extreme New Testament):

"King Jesus, I want to dwell in the SECRET PLACE of the Most High. I want to abide under the shadow of the Almighty. Lord, You are my refuge and my fortress; my God, in You I will trust.

Today, Lord, I hear the words that You said to Your disciples, and I apply them to my own life: "Let us go away to a quiet place to be alone. We can relax a little." I want that. I want to learn to go to a quiet place and be alone with You. I want to really know what it means to relax and experience Your peace.

Bless the children of our church today. Help them learn to spend time with You in the Secret Place. Amen."

**Welcome
15 minutes**

 CANDY RAPPERS *(Enter running)*

CHEER: "Unloading Cheer!"

 SONGS: "I'm Loved by God"; "More, More, More"

 LEADER *(After welcoming the children)*: Boys and girls, today's lesson is called, **"Choose to Forgive."** We are going to begin by standing together and saying what is known as **"The Lord's Prayer."** You might notice that a few extra words have been added. We will discuss these later.

Read together the Overhead Transparency Week Four: "The Lord's Prayer…and Beyond."

LEADER: Hmm …forgive us our trespasses (that means our sins—everything we do that is wrong) AS—**in exactly the same way**—we forgive those who trespass (that means their sins—everything they do that is wrong) against us. Have you ever thought about that before? And look at the last two verses: "For if ye forgive men their trespasses, your heavenly Father will also forgive you: But if ye forgive not men their trespasses, neither will your Father forgive your trespasses."

Do you think that's true? *(Allow discussion)* God's Word is true. He means what He says; and He says what He means! In fact, God says four times in the gospels that He will forgive us IF we forgive other people! (See Matthew 6:14-15; 18:35; Mark 11:26; Luke 6:37.) **It sounds like forgiveness is very important to the Lord.**

Sometimes I've heard of children saying things like: "No! I won't forgive you! I'll never be your friend again!" How does the Bible say that God will forgive us? (In exactly the same way we forgive other people.) **How would you feel if the next time you said, "Jesus, forgive my sins," He answered back with: "No! I won't forgive you! I'll never be your friend again!"** A scary thought, isn't it?

Memory Verse
10 minutes

KINGDOM RUNNER comes running in, wearing workout clothing. He runs around the room, then comes to the front and motions for the children to stand and begin running on the spot.

KINGDOM RUNNER: "Hello, Young God Chasers! How is your chase going? Are you running toward King Jesus with all your heart?! One very heavy burden that will slow you down is UNFORGIVENESS. Get rid of it! You already read what Jesus said about forgiveness in Matthew chapter 6. This is what Ephesians 4:32 teaches about forgiveness: "Have tender feelings and be kind to one another. Forgive one another just as God, in Christ, forgave you." *(Ephesians 4:32 GCENT)*

Teach the Hugga-Wugga™ paraphrase *(Hear the rhythm on the CD)*

Memory Verse #1
"From Matthew chapter 6: The Lord's Prayer...and beyond...
Lord, forgive my sins in exactly the same way
I choose to forgive other people."

Memory Verse #2
"Be kind to one another
Tenderhearted
Forgiving one another
'Cause God's forgiven you!
Ephesians 4 verse-32!"

Memory Verse #1

WORDS	ACTIONS
"From Matthew chapter 6: The Lord's Prayer...	*Look at an invisible open Bible you are holding*
and beyond...	*Look forward*
Lord, forgive my sins in exactly the same way	*Turn slightly right; reach up with both hands and receive forgiveness from the Lord into your heart*
I choose to forgive other people."	*Turn slightly left; reach out with both hands and offer forgiveness to another person*

Memory Verse #2

Memory Verse #2

WORDS	ACTIONS
"Be kind to one another	*With a partner—clap own hands, their hands, left, right, own and repeat to the beat.*
Tenderhearted	
Forgiving one another	
'Cause God's forgiven you!	
Ephesians 4	
verse-32!"	*Clap own hands then slap sides sharply*

REMEMBER.....
Continue to review memory verses from previous lessons.

A Narrated Skit "The Unforgiving Servant" (See Matthew 18:22-35)

Creative Illustration 25 minutes

Characters: NARRATOR; then choose children from the audience to be the KING, SERVANT, GEORGE and ALBERT. Put simple costumes on them—just hats are fun! The characters simply act out the narration. Ad-libbing is encouraged!
Props: Chair for the king's throne.

Put the hats/costumes on each character and introduce them; then KING and SERVANT wait at the front off to the side. GEORGE and ALBERT sit on opposite sides of the room among the audience. The audience is the town where they live.

NARRATOR: One day Jesus' disciples asked Him how many times they should forgive people—seven times? Jesus' answer surprised the disciples. He told them to forgive seventy times seven times! And then Jesus told a story that went something like this...

NARRATOR	ACTIONS
Once there lived a king.	***KING*** and ***SERVANT*** enter. ***KING*** sits on his "throne."

continued

Creative Illustration cont.
"The Unforgiving Servant"

NARRATOR	ACTIONS
The king looked through his royal record book of the people who owed him money.	**KING** *flips the pages of an invisible book while echoing the* **NARRATOR'S** *lines.*
"Hmm, _____ *(Insert the name of someone the children know)* owes me $100."	*Hmm, _____ owes me $100.*
"_____ *(Insert the name of someone the children know)* owes me $5,000."	*_____ owes me $5,000.*
"_____ *(Insert the name of someone the children know)* owes me $25,000.00."	*_____ owes me $25,000.00.*
"WHAT?! This says that a man named George owes me TEN MILLION dollars!"	*WHAT?! This says that a man named George owes me TEN MILLION dollars!*
"Servant!"	*Servant!*
"Yes, Your Highness?"	*Yes, Your Highness?*
"Find George and bring him to me!"	*Find George and bring him to me!*
"Yes sir, Your Highness!"	*Yes sir, Your Highness!*
The servant went out into the town, looking for George…He looked, and looked, and looked, until he finally found him.	**SERVANT** *"searches," asking people in the "town" (the audience) where George lives; finally finds* **GEORGE**.
"George! The king wants to see you right away!"	*George! The king wants to see you right away!*
"Uh-oh," said George. "I owe the king a LOT of money! Uh-Oh."	*Uh-oh, said George. I owe the king a LOT of money! Uh-Oh.*
The king's servant took George to the king.	**SERVANT** *takes* **GEORGE** *to the* **KING**.
When they arrived, George fell down at the king's feet.	**GEORGE** *falls down at* **KING'S** *feet.*
The king said, "George, you owe me ten million dollars! When do you intend to pay me?"	*George, you owe me ten million dollars! When do you intend to pay me?*

continued

Creative Illustration cont.
"The Unforgiving Servant"

NARRATOR	ACTIONS
George cried out to the king.	
"Please, Your Highness!	*Please, Your Highness!*
Give me a bit more time!	*Give me a bit more time!*
I'll pay it all back—I promise!"	*I'll pay it all back—I promise!*
The king shook his head.	***KING*** *shakes head.*
"George, you know what the law says.	*George, you know what the law says.*
If a man cannot pay his debts, he is to be sold as a slave!"	*If a man cannot pay his debts, he is to be sold as a slave!*
George begged the king for mercy and cried out with a loud voice.	
"Please, King! Have mercy!	*Please, King! Have mercy!*
I have the wife, and the kids!	*I have the wife, and the kids!*
The mortgage payment!	*The mortgage payment!*
The car payment!	*The car payment!*
I'll pay it all back—please, just give me more time! Please! Please have mercy!"	*I'll pay it all back—please, just give me more time! Please! Please have mercy!*
The king thought about it.	***KING*** *thinks about it.*
He asked his servant for his royal record book.	***SERVANT*** *hands "book" to* ***KING***.
"All right, George, I WILL have mercy!	*All right, George, I WILL have mercy!*
Look, I will erase your debt!	*Look, I will erase your debt!*
You no longer owe me anything! Your debt has been forgiven!"	*(****KING**** "erases" the debt from his book.)*
	You no longer owe me anything! Your debt has been forgiven!
George was surprised and thankful.	*George acts surprised and thankful.*
George was VERY surprised and thankful.	*George acts VERY surprised and thankful.*

continued

Creative Illustration cont.
"The Unforgiving Servant"

NARRATOR	ACTIONS
Then George went out into the streets of the town telling everyone what the king had done for him.	**GEORGE** *goes up and down the aisles of the audience, the "town," calling:*
"Hey, everyone! The king is wonderful!	*Hey, everyone! The king is wonderful!*
The king forgave me a debt I could NEVER have repaid!	*The king forgave me a debt I could NEVER have repaid!*
What a wonderful king we serve!"	*What a wonderful king we serve!*
Just then, George saw his friend, Albert.	**GEORGE** *sees* **ALBERT**.
"Hey! There's Albert!	*Hey! There's Albert!*
Albert owes me twenty dollars!	*Albert owes me twenty dollars!*
I wonder when he's going to pay me back?!"	*I wonder when he's going to pay me back?!*
George went over to Albert and asked him about the debt.	
"Hey! Albert! You owe me twenty dollars!	*Hey! Albert! You owe me twenty dollars!*
When are you going to pay me back?!"	*When are you going to pay me back?!*
Albert cried out to George.	
"Please, George!	*Please, George!*
Give me a bit more time!	*Give me a bit more time!*
I'll pay it all back—I promise!"	*I'll pay it all back—I promise!*
George grabbed Albert by the collar and said,	**GEORGE** *grabs* **ALBERT** *at the collar and says,*
"Albert, you know what the law says.	*Albert, you know what the law says.*
If a man cannot pay his debts, he is to be sold as a slave!"	*If a man cannot pay his debts, he is to be sold as a slave!*
Albert begged George for mercy and cried out with a loud voice.	
"Please, George! Have mercy!	*Please, George! Have mercy!*
I have the wife, and the kids!	*I have the wife, and the kids!*

continued

Creative Illustration cont.
"The Unforgiving Servant"

NARRATOR	ACTIONS
The mortgage payment!	*The mortgage payment!*
The car payment!	*The car payment!*
I'll pay it all back—please, just give me more time! Please! Please have mercy!"	*I'll pay it all back—please, just give me more time! Please! Please have mercy!*
But George shook his head.	***GEORGE*** *shakes his head.*
"No way, Albert! Listen, today the King forgave me a debt I could never have repaid.	*No way, Albert! Listen, today the king forgave me a debt I could never have repaid.*
Lucky for me!	*Lucky for me!*
But if I would have had that twenty dollars you owe me, I could have at least given that to the king!"	*But if I would have had that twenty dollars you owe me, I could have at least given that to the king!*
Just then, the king's servant was taking a walk through town.	***SERVANT*** *walks quite near and listens to what* ***GEORGE*** *says to* ***ALBERT***.
He overheard what George said to Albert.	
"Listen, Albert!	*Listen, Albert!*
You need to learn to pay your debts!	*You need to learn to pay your debts!*
I'm going to have you thrown into prison until you can pay that twenty dollars back to me!"	*I'm going to have you thrown into prison until you can pay that twenty dollars back to me!*
George threw Albert into prison while Albert begged for mercy.	***GEORGE*** *throws* ***ALBERT*** *into the corner of the room while Albert continues to beg for mercy.*
And the king's servant felt very sad. He went and told the king what had happened.	***KING'S SERVANT*** *sadly goes to the* ***KING*** *and tells him what happened.*
The king was shocked.	***KING*** *acts very shocked.*
"What?!" he cried. "Servant, bring George to me!"	*What?!*
	Servant, bring George to me!
Meanwhile, George was still out in the streets of the town telling everyone what the king had done for him.	***GEORGE*** *goes up and down the aisles calling:*

continued

Creative Illustration cont.
"The Unforgiving Servant"

NARRATOR	ACTIONS
"Hey, everyone! The king is wonderful!	*Hey, everyone! The king is wonderful!*
The king forgave me a debt I could NEVER have repaid!	*The king forgave me a debt I could NEVER have repaid!*
What a wonderful king we serve!"	*What a wonderful king we serve!*
The king's servant told George the king wanted to see him again.	***SERVANT***: *George! The king wants to see you again!*
George felt a little nervous as he went to kneel before the king.	***GEORGE*** *bites his fingernails nervously as he goes to kneel before the king.*
The king was angry.	***KING*** *acts angry.*
The Bible says that he was VERY angry! *(See Matthew 18:34.)*	***KING*** *acts VERY angry.*
The king said, "George, you evil man! You begged me, so I forgave your whole debt! You should have given mercy to Albert like I gave mercy to you!	*George, you evil man! You begged me, so I forgave your whole debt! You should have given mercy to Albert like I gave mercy to you!*
And the king handed George over to be punished until he paid back everything he owed.	***SERVANT*** *takes **GEORGE** and throws him into the prison and releases **ALBERT**.*

LEADER *(After thanking the NARRATOR and the children who acted out the story,)* That skit was based on a parable that Jesus told. Jesus often told simple stories to teach very important truth. **I want to read the last part of what Jesus said right from the Bible**, in Matthew chapter 18:

"Then the master of the first servant came to him and said, 'You evil servant! You begged me, so I canceled your whole debt. You should have given mercy to your fellow servant as I did to you!' The master became very angry. He handed the servant over to some men to punish him, until he paid back everything he owed. My heavenly Father will treat you the same way, if each of you does not forgive his brother or sister from his heart." *(Matthew 18:32-35 GCENT)*

"My heavenly Father will treat you the same way, if each of you does not forgive his brother or sister from his heart." We must choose to forgive. We need King Jesus to help us.

Secret Place Time 20 minutes

LEADER: Boys and girls, today's lesson is called, "Choose to Forgive." If you choose NOT to forgive people, there are consequences. Unforgiveness is a very heavy burden that far too many people carry for years and years. Let it go. **Give that burden to Jesus and CHOOSE to forgive. If you will make that choice, King Jesus will be right there to help you!**

Let's go into the Secret Place right now and talk to Jesus about any burdens of unforgiveness we have been carrying…

Please close your eyes. **Throughout today's lesson, have you been thinking about someone who has hurt you in some way?** Maybe a family member, or a teacher, or perhaps a bully at school…or maybe, it is someone right here in this room. Whoever it is, **I invite you right now to CHOOSE to forgive them. Or maybe YOU have been the one who has hurt someone with your words or actions and you need to ask someone to forgive you.**

I will lead you in a prayer, and then we will spend some quiet time with King Jesus. **If the person who has hurt you is here today, or if you have hurt someone here—after we pray, it would be a very good thing for you to go to that person and talk to them.**

Please put your hand on your heart and pray after me:

"King Jesus, *(children echo)* thank You for forgiving me. *(children echo)* Please help me to forgive other people. *(children echo)* Lord, You see the person *(children echo)* or the people *(children echo)* who have hurt me *(children echo)* with what they said *(children echo)* or what they did. *(children echo)* I give you the pain that they caused. *(children echo)* I give it to You, Lord. *(children echo)* And today, I make a choice. *(children echo)* I choose to forgive them. *(children echo)* And now that I've made that choice *(children echo)* I ask you to help me to really do it! *(children echo)* Give me the ability *(children echo)* to really and truly forgive *(children echo)* just like You really and truly forgive me *(children echo)* for all the wrong things I've done in my life. *(children echo)* And King Jesus, *(children echo)* I ask You to please bless them. *(children echo)* Heal their hearts from hurts *(children echo)* so they won't hurt other people anymore *(children echo)* with their words or actions. *(children echo)* And one more thing, Lord. *(children echo)* please help ME *(children echo)* to ask forgiveness of any people *(children echo)* who I have hurt *(children echo)* with my words or actions. *(children echo)* Amen."

Gently encourage the children to go to anyone in the room they need to either forgive or to ask forgiveness of. If the person is not there, encourage them to go to whoever it is this week and talk to them.

Ask the Lord how to close the meeting. Be sensitive to the children. Some might need an extended time of prayer. In that case, assign workers to remain with those children while the others go to Small Group Time.

Small Group Time

Small Group
20 minutes

GOD'S WORD

Look up these verses and discuss what they mean in the lives of the children this week.

TODAY'S MEMORY VERSES: Matthew 6:12,14-15 -
Forgive me AS I forgive other people.
Ephesians 4:32 - *Be kind to one another and forgive.*

Matthew 6: 9-13 - *The Lord's Prayer.*
Matthew 18:21-22 - *Forgive seventy times seven times.*
Matthew 18:22-35 - *Jesus told the parable of the unforgiving servant.*
Mark 11:25-26 - *When you stand praying, forgive.*
Matthew 6:14-15; 18:35; Mark 11:26 - *If you want God to forgive you, you MUST forgive other people.*
Luke 23:34; Hebrews 12:3 - *Think about what Jesus had to suffer, and He still chose to forgive!*

TALK ABOUT IT TIME
Discuss the following points from today's story:

- **You don't have to tell us out loud, but have you ever said: "No! I won't forgive you! I'll never be your friend again!" After hearing today's lesson, do you think that you will ever say that again?**

- **Have you ever had someone say something like that to you? How did you feel?**

- **When people say or do mean things to us, we can feel that we have a right to unforgiveness. At times like that, we need to think about how Jesus was treated; and how He chose to respond.** *(Discuss how Jesus was treated and how He chose to respond.)*

SOMEONE IN THE BIBLE WHO CHOSE TO FORGIVE
Luke 23:34 - Jesus

TOGETHER IN THE SECRET PLACE
(Not many adult prayers, please—let the children pray!)
Ask King Jesus to help you be more like Him—when you are treated unfairly to choose to forgive. Pray for any bullies at school, or any prayer requests the children have, particularly situations they are in where it is hard to forgive.

DOOR HANGER

Duplicate for the children to cut out and take home. Encourage them to hang up this week's door hanger on their bedroom doorknob when they are spending time with King Jesus in the SECRET PLACE.

Shh! I'm with King Jesus in the Secret Place

MEMORY VERSES:
Matthew 6; Ephesians 4:32
(Hugga Wugga™ Paraphrase)

"From Matthew chapter 6:
The Lord's Prayer…and beyond…
Lord, forgive my sins in exactly the same way
I choose to forgive other people."

"Be kind to one another
Tenderhearted
Forgiving one another
'Cause God's forgiven you!
Ephesians 4 verse - 32!"

THE LORD'S PRAYER... AND BEYOND
(Matthew 6:9-15 KJV, with slight modifications)

Our Father which art in heaven, Hallowed be thy name.

Thy kingdom come. Thy will be done in earth, as it is in heaven.

Give us this day our daily bread.

And forgive us our trespasses (that means our sins—everything we do that is wrong) AS—**in exactly the same way**—we forgive those who trespass and sin against us.

And lead us not into temptation, but deliver us from evil: For thine is the kingdom, and the power, and the glory, for ever. Amen.

For if ye forgive men their trespasses (that means your sins—everything you do that is wrong), your heavenly Father will also forgive you:

But if ye forgive not men their trespasses (that means their sins—everything they do that is wrong), neither will your Father forgive your trespasses (that means your sins—everything you do that is wrong).

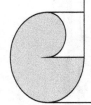

Seeker's SECRET PLACE

Week #5:
"The Holy Spirit:
Teacher, Helper, Comforter"

MEMORY VERSES:
John 7:38-39
(Hugga Wugga™ Paraphrase)

*"The Holy Spirit is a lot like a River
Of water that is ALIVE!
Flow in and out of ME, Holy Spirit
That's John chapter 7:38 and 39"*

Secret Sources of Power Quotes

Page 9 - From *Secret Sources of Power*

… when you unload your own preconceived notions of power and responsibility and give yourself to Christ, the Holy Spirit is released by you and through you.

Pages 11-12 - From *Secret Sources of Power*

…we must realize that before there can be a filling, there has to be an emptying. It is hard for God to fill a person who is already running over with "self." He can't give you solutions when you are clinging to your problems and refuse to unload them.

Pages 27-28 - From *Secret Sources of Power*

The 120 people who gathered together in the Upper Room in Acts chapter 1 had a lot of things to unload, and it seems that Jesus knew that. He specifically said, "Behold, I send the Promise of My Father upon you; but tarry in the city of Jerusalem until you are endued with power from on high" (Lk. 24:49). The Greek word translated as *tarry* means to "sit down, settle, and continue."

What exactly did those people do in the Upper Room? They waited on the Lord and they *unloaded* every preconceived notion of what they thought God was going to do. They put aside every offense that could separate them and destroy their unity. The seven to ten days the 120 spent unloading in prayer and fasting was followed *by an instantaneous in-filling* of the Holy Spirit! It is time for us to visit the Upper Room again. We need to unload every weight and encumbrance so He can "on-load" His Spirit in power and glory!

WEEK #5: "The Holy Spirit: Teacher, Helper, Comforter"

Leader's "PRAYERparation"
Please take time to thoroughly read this lesson, as well as the front pages of this curriculum, well in advance of your teaching time.

The Holy Spirit: Teacher, Helper, Comforter
The Scripture tells us to be filled with the Holy Spirit. If we are filled up with sin, pain, shame, or guilt; or with worries, cares and problems, we are very limited to how much room we have to be filled with the Holy Spirit! Please open your heart and receive His ministry in your midst. **He wants to be Teacher, Helper, and Comforter to you**, and to the children.

Foundational Scriptures for This Lesson. *Please Read Them...*

John 14:26 - *The Holy Spirit is our Teacher.*
Romans 8:26-27 - *The Holy Spirit is our Helper.*
John 16:7 - *The Holy Spirit is our Comforter.*
1 John 5:7 - *The Holy Spirit is GOD!*
Ephesians 5:18; Acts 13:52 - *Be filled with the Holy Spirit.*
Acts 2:39 - *This promise is for you and for your children.*
Luke 11:13 - *The Father will give the Holy Spirit to those who ask Him.*

Today's Memory Verse:
John 7:37-39 - *Rivers of Living Water!*

Order of Activities (Suggested)

 5 min — Welcome
Cheer: "Unloading" with CANDY RAPPERS

 10 min — Creative Illustration
Object Lesson "Filled Up" Part A

 5 min — Memory Verse
(with SPIRIT-MAN)

 5 min — Creative Illustration
"David's Secret Place"
Songs: "The Holy Spirit Song"; "More, More, More"

 15 min — Creative Illustration
"Preacher From Southwest of Somewhere"

 30 min — Secret Place Time
Songs: "In the Secret Place"; "My Hiding Place"

 20 min — Small Group Time

To maximize the effectiveness of this lesson, here is a **SUGGESTED LIST** of materials:

- DAVID Costume
- CANDY RAPPERS Costumes
- SPIRIT-MAN Costume
- THE PREACHER Costume
- Holy Spirit overhead transparencies
- Materials for Object Lesson
- Wrapped Candy
- **Basics** - Overhead projector, Transparencies, CD Player, Name tags, Bibles, Small Group Pages, Secret Place Doorknob Verse

WEEK #5: "The Holy Spirit: Teacher, Helper, Comforter"

Leader & Small Group Leaders
PRAY FOR THE CHILDREN *before they come into the room today*, .

This prayer is based on John 7:38-39 *(God Chasers Extreme New Testament)*:

"King Jesus, You said that the person who believes in You will have a river of fresh water flowing out from his being. You were talking about the Holy Spirit. Today, we will be talking about the Holy Spirit…and as we do, we pray that we will not just talk about, but that we will EXPERIENCE who the Holy Spirit is! We pray that the children will have an encounter today with Your Spirit: Teacher, Helper, Comforter, and "Filler-Upper." We pray that the children will have a new appreciation and understanding of the Holy Spirit: GOD! We welcome You, the Holy Spirit. Come and be who You ARE in our midst today. We welcome and anticipate Your ministry. Amen."

Welcome
5 minutes

CANDY RAPPERS *(Enter running)*
CHEER: "Unloading"

LEADER *(After greeting the children)*: For the past few weeks we have been learning about unloading our burdens on the Lord. Today, we will tell you a very important reason why we must unload our burdens on the Lord. And we're not going to just tell you! We will SHOW you!

Creative Illustration
10 minutes

Object Lesson "Filled Up" Part A

Need: A plastic table cloth in case of spills. Two identical glass water pitchers. One is full of dirt, junk, and water colored with a combination of blue, green, and yellow food coloring to make an ugly, murky shade. The other pitcher is clean and empty. If at all possible, connect a hose to a water faucet and screw a nozzle on the end of it. This will signify an unending source of water. If this is not possible, just use a large bottle of water.

Ask a child to come and fill the dirty, junky pitcher with water. The child will obviously not be able to do that.

LEADER Boys and girls, looking at this problem here, who can tell me the **very important reason we must unload our burdens on the Lord?** *(Allow discussion. Gently steer the responses to something like: "The hose is ready to fill the pitcher with an endless supply of clean fresh water. The pitcher doesn't have room to receive it because it is too full of junk!")*

Creative Illustration cont.
"Filled Up"

LEADER God's Spirit is always ready to fill us with life and power! We MUST unload our burdens—our sin, pain, shame, or guilt; our troubles, worries, fears, and problems. They take up way too much room inside of us! And what does King Jesus WANT us to be filled with? (Joy, happiness, peace, HIM!...) **If you are full of heavy burdens, there's not room for much of JESUS in you!** He gets all squished into a little area but He wants to FILL you with Himself!

Now ask a child to come and fill the clean, empty pitcher with water. Let it overflow slightly onto the plastic cloth.

LEADER **If we are like the clean, empty pitcher and the hose is like the Holy Spirit's unending flow of life and power, what do you think happens when we overflow?** (Allow discussion. Gently steer the responses to something like, "It is GOOD to be filled and overflowing with the Holy Spirit! Then we can splash the people around us! That is MUCH better than splashing people with junk from inside us!")

Memory Verse
5 minutes

SPIRIT-MAN *(Enters excitedly)* Hi, everyone! I know a REALLY great memory verse about that! It's SO important!!! It will help you all for the rest of your life—believe me! It's found in the King's Great Book. John 7:37-39 in the God Chasers Extreme New Testament says:

On the last and most important day of the festival, Jesus stood and cried out, "If you are thirsty, come to Me and drink! The person who believes in Me will be like the Scripture which says: 'A river of fresh water will flow from his body.'" *(Here Jesus was talking about the Spirit whom the believers were about to receive. The Spirit had not yet been given, because Jesus had not yet been raised to glory.)*

Teach the Hugga-Wugga™ paraphrase *(Hear the rhythm on the CD)*

"The Holy Spirit is a lot like a River
Of water that is ALIVE!
Flow in and out of ME, Holy Spirit
That's John chapter 7:38 and 39"

WORDS	ACTIONS
"The Holy Spirit is a lot like a River	*Country style! Both hands slightly in front pants*
Of water that is ALIVE!	*pockets and lean right then left on the beat and*
Flow in and out of ME, Holy Spirit	*speak with an exaggerated drawl.*
That's John chapter 7:38 and 39"	

Memory Verse cont.

LEADER *(After thanking SPIRIT-MAN)* Wow! God's Spirit sounds like Someone we need to get to know better!

REMEMBER.....
Continue to review memory verses from previous lessons.

Creative Illustration 5 minutes

"David's Secret Place"

DAVID is dressed like a shepherd boy. He has a slingshot hanging from his back pocket. He enters, reading Psalms 31:2-3 in a melodic voice.

This is a "Kids In Ministry Opportunity!"

DAVID "Turn Your ear to me, come quickly to my rescue; be my rock of refuge, a strong fortress to save me. Since You are my rock and my fortress, for the sake of Your name lead and guide me." *(Psalms 31:2-3 NIV)*

LEADER Excuse me, David? Sorry to interrupt your Secret Place time…you are someone who REALLY knew the Spirit of God. Could you tell me three words you would use to describe who He is?

DAVID *(Thinks for a moment)* Just three?! There are thousands of words to describe who He is! But just three—well, I suppose I would say He is my Teacher, my Helper, and my Comforter. *(He exits, reading aloud.)*

"I will instruct you and teach you in the way you should go;
I will counsel you and watch over you." (Psalms 32:8 NIV)

 SONGS: "The Holy Spirit Song"; "More, More, More"

Creative Illustration 15 minutes

Preacher From Southwest of Somewhere: "Who Is the Holy Spirit?"

This is a "Kids In Ministry Opportunity!"

THE PREACHER wears a simple costume—like a vest and tie— and carries a BIG Bible. He must be energetic, bold, excited about Jesus, and FUN! He should talk with a country drawl, emphasizing all words that are typed in bold. Allow response times between the lines. Go ahead and use the sermon notes. Highlight the key lines. Make lots of eye contact with the children. Be sure to stay in character during the entire script.

Creative Illustration cont.
"Who Is the Holy Spirit?"

Small Group Leaders and Helpers—work with the children to find the Bible verses. Also help the Preacher by saying things like, "Amen!" "Thank You, Jesus!" "That's RIGHT!" "Preach it!"

*The PREACHER has a bag of wrapped candy for the Small Group Leaders to hand out during the sermon. He also has Holy Spirit overhead transparency pictures.

PREACHER: Hallelujah! MM-MMM! How I LOVE the Holy Spirit! That thare song you all were jest singing is mighty fine; yes, a MIGHTY FINE song!

Howdy! I'm just so glad to be here! I'm the PREACHER From Southwest of Somewhere!

I'm mighty pleased, yes, MIGHTY PLEASED at what they are teachin' you young 'uns around here! It's about TIME somebody started telling you kids about UNLOADING all yer heavy burdens so you can get FILLED RIGHT UP FULL of the power of God! Hallelujah! It's time to learn more about the HOLY SPIRIT!

Do you have yer BIBLES? Alright then, open them up to Luke chapter 11, verse 13. Stick yer finger in there to mark the spot and turn on over to Acts chapter 2, verse 38.

I brought along with me here today some of them thare overhead transparency pictures to show you all so you can "get the picture" about WHO the Holy Spirit of God is! Alright now, picture number 1!

PICTURE #1: Holy Spirit Gift Box

Jesus said that He would send the Holy Spirit to us.

Have a child read Acts 2:38.

That was MIGHY FINE readin'! Thare it is! God's Great Book says the Holy Spirit is a GIFT.

Have a child read Luke 11:13.

That was some MORE mighty fine readin'! We're to ASK and God will give us the GIFT of His Holy Spirit. Hallelujah! MM-MMM! How I LOVE the Holy Spirit!

PICTURE # 2: Holy Spirit Gift Box in Heart

When you ASK God for His gift, He GIVES you the gift! And you HAVE the Holy Spirit! And believe me, your inner SPIRIT-MAN really LIKES this GIFT!

Now, I jest so happened to bring along a little gift myself today! I have in this here bag some CANDY! Do you LIKE candy? I thought so! Well, I'm gonna give some handfuls of this here candy to the Small Group leaders and on account of my sermon today being a bit long—I'm asking for you leader folks to slip these here boys and

continued

Creative Illustration cont.
"Who Is the Holy Spirit?"

girls a bit of candy whenever you happen to see them sittin' up nice and straight and payin' attention!

PICTURE # 3: Open Box

The Holy Spirit has LOTS of GOOD things for you. The past few weeks you've been learning about giving all your burdens to Jesus—to unload all your trouble and concern—so you will have room inside your heart for all the GOOD things God's Spirit has for you. When you are filled with the Holy Spirit, get ready for ADVENTURE! Say it with me—Hallelujah! MM-MMM! How I LOVE the Holy Spirit!

PICTURE # 4: Reading the Bible

Alright now, please turn in yer BIBLES to the Book of John, chapter 14 verse 26. *(Have a child read this.)*

The Holy Spirit is our TEACHER! Hallelujah! He teaches you about Jesus and brings back to your mind what God has said in His Word. The Holy Spirit teaches us how to live for Jesus; He guides us into all truth.

Say it with me—Hallelujah! MM-MMM! How I LOVE the Holy Spirit!

PICTURE # 5: Direct Line

Let's go on over to the Book of Romans. That's right after John, right after Acts… there it is, Romans! Okay, turn to chapter 8 verses 26 and 27.

(Have a child read Romans 8:26-27.)

The Holy Spirit is your HELPER! He helps you and helps you and helps you! And one very important WAY He helps you is when you PRAY. Kids, did you know that you have a 24-HOUR TOLL-FREE OPEN LINE to Heaven?! HALLELUJAH! Jude 20 talks about praying IN the Spirit. That just means letting the Holy Spirit pray through you.

Say it with me—Hallelujah! MM-MMM! How I LOVE the Holy Spirit!

PICTURE # 6: Holy Spirit Prayer

Romans chapter 8 says that we don't KNOW HOW to pray like we should. The Holy Spirit wants to pray THROUGH you. And when the Holy Spirit prays, He prays exactly the right prayer! This is how the God Chasers Extreme New Testament says it: "We don't KNOW HOW we should pray, but the Spirit HELPS our weakness. He personally talks to God for us with feelings which our language cannot express."

continued

Creative Illustration cont.
"Who Is the Holy Spirit?"

Some versions say "with groanings that words cannot express."

Sometimes it's peaceful…sometimes it's loud…and sometimes there is a kind of groaning that comes out…Just TRUST the Holy Spirit and pray WITH Him! Say it with me—Hallelujah! MM-MMM! How I LOVE the Holy Spirit!

PICTURE # 7: Tuned In

The Holy Spirit will HELP your SPIRIT-MAN get "tuned in" to God. The Holy Spirit will TEACH you how to pray and what to say. He will SHOW you what you need to KNOW; and He will SHOW you the way to GO. He will direct your life. Say it with me—Hallelujah! MM-MMM! How I LOVE the Holy Spirit!

I know you younguns have been crying out to the Lord to take yer heavy burdens. The Holy Spirit wants to HELP you do that! He also wants to help you pray for other folks 'cause we just don't know what people need; but the Holy Spirit knows EXACTLY what they need! And He will HELP us pray! Hallelujah!

The Holy Spirit is yer TEACHER, yer HELPER, and—the Holy Spirit is yer COMFORTER!

Alright now—we're appoachin' the end of my sermon! How's that CANDY holdin' out? Do ya still have some to give to these here children fer being so ATTENTIVE? Good! Now, please turn in yer BIBLES to John chapter 16, verse 7. Jesus was telling His disciples that He was going to go back to Heaven… *(Have a child read John 16:7)*

PICTURE # 8: Comforter

Jesus promised to send the COMFORTER! Hallelujah! Do any of you boys and girls have a nice cozy BLANKET you like to wrap yerself up in? That's what's called a comforter—and the Holy Spirit is a lot like that! He WRAPS YOU UP and COMFORTS you! like them thare words of the song you were all singing a bit ago: "Wrap me up in Your presence, Oh, God."

Say it with me—Hallelujah! MM-MMM! How I LOVE the Holy Spirit! I feel the Comforter right here and now! Okay, one more fact about WHO the Holy Spirit is!

PICTURE # 9: Love, Joy, and Peace

(Have a child read Acts 13:52 and Ephesians 5:18)

Don't be drunk with wine—that will RUIN your life! Let me tell it to you straight, younguns. The reason some folks drink alcohol and take drugs is because they have a NEED inside. They NEED to feel GOOD. I'll tell you how to get feeling good inside! It's the NEW WINE of the Holy Spirit, the LIVING WATER! Get filled up with Him and you'll feel GOOD, let me tell ya!

continued

Creative Illustration cont.
"Who Is the Holy Spirit?"

HALLELUJAH! He wants you to be FILLED to OVERFLOWING! The Holy Spirit is like a RIVER—and He wants to OVERFLOW and spill out through your life! Jest like that thare HUGGA-WUGGA™ memory verse you learned earlier today—

"The Holy Spirit is a lot like a River
Of water that is ALIVE!
Flow in and out of ME, Holy Spirit
That's John chapter 7:38 and 39"

He is my TEACHER, my HELPER, my COMFORTER, and my FILLER-UPPER! He is the Holy Spirit of ALMIGHTY GOD! Say it with me—Hallelujah! MM-MMM! How I LOVE the Holy Spirit!

PICTURE # 1: Holy Spirit Gift Box

And kids, you NEED to be FILLED up FULL and OVERFLOWING with the HOLY SPIRIT! Ask God for His WONDERFUL GIFT today! HALLELUJAH!

LEADER Wow! **Thanks SO MUCH** for sharing this with us, PREACHER! Before you go back to Southwest of Somewhere, would you stay and sing **the Holy Spirit song** again?

PREACHER I'd be mighty glad to do that! It's one of my favorites!

 SONGS: "The Holy Spirit Song"; "More, More, More"

SECRET PLACE TIME

Secret Place Time
30 minutes

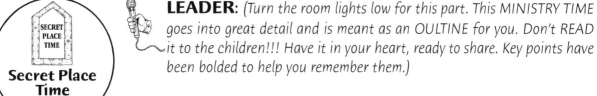
LEADER: *(Turn the room lights low for this part. This MINISTRY TIME goes into great detail and is meant as an OUTLINE for you. Don't READ it to the children!!! Have it in your heart, ready to share. Key points have been bolded to help you remember them.)*

In a few moments, we will pray for every person here today who wants to receive more of what God has to give to you. "This promise is for you and for your CHILDREN!" Those words are in the Bible—in Acts 2:39.

King Jesus wants **all of His followers to be FILLED to overflowing** with all He has for them! **Instead of being filled with sin, pain, shame, or guilt; or troubles, worries, fears, and problems—be filled with God's Spirit!** He wants the clear, pure, powerful River of the Holy Spirit to **fill us and overflow** on everyone around us!

Please stand to your feet. **When you ASK God for the Holy Spirit, what happens?** *(You GET the Holy Spirit! See Luke 11:9-13.)*

Secret Place Time cont.

Okay—if you REALLY want to receive the gift of the Holy Spirit, if you want to be filled to over-flowing with Him, I want you to come up here to the front where we can pray for you. Please do not come up here because your friend comes up or because you think this would be fun. Please only come if you are seriously wanting to **receive the GIFT of the Holy Spirit.**

Right now, this area at the front will be a Secret Place where we can all go together. Here's what we'll do. **I will lead you in a prayer, asking God to fill you with the Holy Spirit; to give you MORE of HIMSELF! Then we will clap and thank Him for doing that! And then we will spend some time with the Holy Spirit.** The Holy Spirit is not an "It"—He is a Person—He is God, the Holy Spirit! And when He comes to you today, He will want to speak to you and touch your life. It is important for us to give Him time to do that! We don't want to rush and say "Fill me with the Holy Spirit. Thanks, good-bye!" No, **we're going to spend some time with Him!**

When you are receiving a gift from someone, the best way to get it is to reach out and take it! It's rather difficult to receive something when your arms are folded or your hands are in your pockets! So, **let's all open our hands to receive while we pray…**

Is there anyone who is wishing you had come forward? It's not too late—you can come right now. And, if for some reason you are not comfortable about coming up front, you don't have to! You can pray with us right where you are sitting! **And if you ASK God for the Holy Spirit what will happen?** *(You will GET the Holy Spirit!)* God will give you MORE of HIMSELF!

Acts 2:38 and 39 says to repent and have Jesus wash away your sins and then you will receive the Gift of the Holy Spirit. Boys and girls, have you all repented of your sins and asked Jesus to forgive you? *(**Have a helper take any unsaved children aside and go through the SPIRIT-MAN booklet with them to explain salvation.**)*

Please bow your heads and pray after me…

When the children come up to the front, have the Small Group Leaders and other helpers come and stand with them, but have some adults remain with the children who did not come forward, encouraging those children to stretch their hands out and pray for the children at the front. Any children you know who are filled with the Spirit should also be invited to help pray.

"Papa God, *(children echo)* Thank You. *(children echo)* Thank You that the promise *(children echo)* of the Holy Spirit *(children echo)* is for everyone—including children! *(children echo)* I want to receive *(children echo)* Your wonderful Gift. *(children echo)* I repent of all my sins *(children echo)* and receive again Your forgiveness. *(children echo)*

Papa God *(children echo)* I believe Your Word. *(children echo)* Your Word says *(children echo)* that if I ask You for the Holy Spirit *(children echo)* You will give me the Holy Spirit! *(children echo)* Today *(children echo)* I ask You for the Holy Spirit. *(children echo)* Fill me with Your Power. *(children echo)* Holy Spirit, be my Teacher. *(children echo))* Be my Helper. *(children echo)* Be my Comforter. *(children echo)* And teach me how to pray. *(children echo)*

Secret Place Time cont.

We welcome you, Holy Spirit. *(children echo)* Thank You SO MUCH for filling us with Your power! *(children echo)* Now we just want to take time to BE with You. *(children echo)* Flow in us, River of God. *(children echo)* Flow through us, River of God. *(children echo)*

Have worship music softly in the background at this point. Small Group leaders and helpers should move quietly among the children—those at the front and those in their chairs—praying softly.

SONGS: "The Holy Spirit Song"; "More, More, More"

MORE for you to share with the children during this time.

Often, in the Bible, when people received God's wonderful Gift, they spoke in what is called, "tongues" or a "heavenly language." Jude 20 says to pray in the Spirit. Romans 8:26 and 27 tells us that we don't know how to pray like we should, and the Holy Spirit will pray through us with deep groans—groans that are so deep no earthly words can express what the Holy Spirit is praying through us.

So, if you ASK God for His Gift of the Holy Spirit today, you will receive a spiritual prayer language. Speaking in your prayer language is part of the package—it comes along with being filled with the Spirit! You don't have to use this language, but you CAN! No one will MAKE you—but you CAN!

The Holy Spirit speaks many languages—words we understand and words we don't understand; deep groanings inside; pictures; dreams; ideas; feelings…Will you let Him speak to you, and THROUGH you however He wants to?

Some people think that children are too young to receive the gift of the Holy Spirit. Listen, John the Baptist was filled with the Holy Spirit while he was in his mother's tummy! *(Luke 1:15, 41)* How much younger could you be?

Small Group Time

**Small Group
20 minutes**

Look up these verses and discuss what they mean in the lives of the children this week.

GOD'S WORD

TODAY'S MEMORY VERSE: John 7:37-39 - Rivers of Living Water!

John 14:26 - The Holy Spirit is our Teacher.
Romans 8:26-27 - The Holy Spirit is our Helper.
John 16:7 - The Holy Spirit is our Comforter.
1 John 5:7 - The Holy Spirit is GOD!
Ephesians 5:18; Acts 13:52 - Be filled with the Holy Spirit.
Acts 2:39 - This promise is for you and for your children.
Luke 11:13 - The Father will give the Holy Spirit to those who ask Him.

TALK ABOUT IT TIME
Discuss the following points from today's story:

- **What did you learn from the water pitcher object lesson?**

- **Who is the Holy Spirit?**

- **Who do you need Him to be in your life right now?**

- **What do you most need Him to fill you up with?**

SOMEONE IN THE BIBLE WHO WAS FILLED UP WITH THE HOLY SPIRIT
Acts 10:44-46; 11:15-17 - Cornelius and his household

TOGETHER IN THE SECRET PLACE
(Not many adult prayers, please—let the children pray!)
If you asked the Holy Spirit to be Teacher, Helper, and Comforter, thank Him! If you didn't come forward for prayer, you can ask Him now! Pray for all the children in your church to be filled with God's Spirit.

* If you have extra time have the kids do the Word Find attached to this lesson or they can take it home.

WORD FIND

(How many ☺ can you find?)

```
H  O  L  Y  S  P  I  R  I  T  G  I  F  T  H
C  O  M  F  O  R  T  E  R  E  P  R  A  Y  O
H  E  L  P  E  R ☺  P  R  A  Y ☺  A  M  L
☺  W ☺  Y  P  R  A  Y ☺  C ☺  R ☺  O  Y
P  R  A  Y  S  Y  A  R  P  H  P  E ☺  R  S
T  A  Y  A  R  P  R  E  S  E  N  C  E  E  P
I  P ☺  J  O  Y  I  P ☺  R ☺  N  P  M  I
R  M  F  I  L  L  E  R  U  P  P  E  R  O  R
I  E ☺ ☺ ☺  C ☺  A  I ☺  R  S  O  R  I
P  U  P  R  A  Y ☺  Y ☺  T  A  E  M  E  T
S  P  R  E  C  E  I  V  E ☺  Y  R  I  M ☺
Y ☺  P  V  J  U  S  T  A  S  K  P  S  O  J
L  I  V  I  N  G  W  A  T  E  R ☺  E  R  O
O  V  E  R  F  L  O  W  I  N  G ☺ ☺  E  Y
H  L  O  V  E  T  I  R  I  P  S  Y  L  O  H
```

COMFORTER	**FILLER UPPER**	**GIFT**
HELPER	**HOLY SPIRIT** (4 times)	**JOY** (2 times)
JUST ASK	**LIVING WATER**	**LOVE**
MORE MORE MORE	**OVERFLOWING**	**PRAY** (7 times)
PRESENCE (2 times)	**PROMISE**	**RECEIVE**
RIVER	**TEACHER**	**WRAP ME UP**

DOOR HANGER

Duplicate for the children to cut out and take home. Encourage them to hang up this week's door hanger on their bedroom doorknob when they are spending time with King Jesus in the SECRET PLACE.

Shh! I'm with King Jesus in the Secret Place

HOLY SPIRIT

MEMORY VERSES:
John 7:38-39
(Hugga Wugga™ Paraphrase)

"The Holy Spirit is a lot like a River
Of water that is ALIVE!
Flow in and out of ME, Holy Spirit
That's John chapter 7:38 and 39"

PICTURE #1: Holy Spirit Gift Box

PICTURE # 2: Holy Spirit Gift Box in Heart

PICTURE # 3: Open Box

PICTURE # 4: Reading the Bible

PICTURE # 5: Direct Line

PICTURE # 6: Holy Spirit Prayer

PICTURE # 7: Tuned In

PICTURE # 8: Comforter

PICTURE # 9: Love, Joy, and Peace

Seeker's SECRET PLACE

Week #6:
"Attitude of Gratitude"

MEMORY VERSES:
Philippians 4:6
(Hugga Wugga™ Paraphrase)

"Don't worry about ANYTHING—Just BE THANKFUL!
Don't worry about ANYTHING—Just BE THANKFUL!
Tell Jesus what you want; tell Jesus what you need
Philippians chapter 4 verse 6—
Always, always be THANKFUL!
Be THANKFUL! Be THANKFUL!"

Secret Sources of Power Quotes

Page 5 - From *Secret Sources of Power*
The Bible says that when Jesus endured the cross, He did it "for the joy that was set before Him…" (Heb. 12:2b). His joy was at least twofold: He anticipated the joy of pleasing His Father, and He anticipated the joy of seeing millions of lost people coming into the Kingdom of God.

Page 62 - From *Secret Sources of Power*
We know that we can create an atmosphere that attracts the Holy Spirit or grieves and repulses Him. God's Word tells us to, "Enter into His gates with thanksgiving, and into His courts with praise. Be thankful to Him, and bless His name" (Ps. 100:4). When we thank the Lord, praise Him, and bless His name, we find ourselves in His presence. It is a question of attitude.

© 2003 Dian Layton   MercyPlace Ministries 77

WEEK #6: "Attitude of Gratitude"

Leader's "PRAYERparation"

Please take time to thoroughly read this lesson, as well as the front pages of this curriculum, well in advance of your teaching time.

Attitude of Gratitude

Grumbling and complaining. Is that something you hear from the children in your church? *(Or from the children's workers?!)* The best weapon against grumbling and complaining is thankfulness. **Today's lesson teaches the importance of having an attitude of gratitude—no matter what is going on around you!** Be forewarned: as you prepare to teach this lesson, you may very well be presented with opportunities to DO what you are about to tell the children to do!

Foundational Scriptures for This Lesson. *Please Read Them...*

Philippians 4:4-7 - *Be thankful and experience God's peace that passes all understanding.*
Psalms 100 - *Be thankful!*
Matthew 5:12 - *Be thankful when people mistreat you!*
1 Peter 1:6 - *Be thankful when life is hard!*
1 Thessalonians 5:16-18 - *Be thankful all the time and in every situation.*
Hebrews 12:2 - *Jesus endured the cross for the joy that was set before Him.*

Today's Memory Verse:
Philippians 4:6 - *Don't worry about anything; just be thankful.*

Order of Activities (Suggested)

10 min   **Memory Verse**
(with the KINGDOM ADMIRAL)
Cheer: "Attitude of Gratitude" with KINGDOM SAILORS

20 min   **Creative Illustration**
"Anointed to Be King"

20 min   **Creative Illustration**
Illustrated Story *In Search of Wanderer*, Part One
Cheer: "Attitude of Gratitude" with KINGDOM SAILORS

20 min   **Secret Place Time**
Song: "I'm Loved by God"

20 min   **Small Group Time**

To maximize the effectiveness
of this lesson, here is a
SUGGESTED LIST of materials:

• KINGDOM SAILORS costume
• KINGDOM ADMIRAL costume
• IDCLARE costume
• MINSTRELS costumes
• DAVID costume
• Paper and pencils
• **Basics** - Overhead projector, Transparencies, CD Player, Name tags, Bibles, Small Group Pages, Secret Place Doorknob Verse

   © 2003 Dian Layton

WEEK #6: "Attitude of Gratitude"

Leader & Small Group Leaders
PRAY FOR THE CHILDREN *before they come into the room today*, .
This prayer is based on 1 Thessalonians 5:15-18 *(God Chasers Extreme New Testament)*:

"King Jesus, You have told us to always be happy in our faith, to pray continually, and to thank You at all times—no matter what our circumstances! You told us to always be glad and not to worry about ANYTHING! Instead, we are to let You know what we are asking for in prayer. We are to tell You all about what we want. And, again, to be thankful. If we do this, You promised that God's peace, which goes far beyond all human understanding, will guard our hearts and minds in Christ Jesus. Lord, we need Your HELP! Help us and help the children to have an attitude of gratitude—all the time!"

Memory Verse
10 minutes

LEADER *(After welcoming the children)* Today we are beginning a new section of the curriculum; and the beginning of a brand new Seeker story called, *In Search of Wanderer.* In a little while we will hear Part One. It is about having an **"attitude of gratitude"** and that is exactly what today's memory verse is about!

KINGDOM ADMIRAL comes marching in, wearing a Navy cap.

KINGDOM ADMIRAL "Aye, Aye, mates! I, I am the KINGDOM ADMIRAL—officer in charge of the King's Royal Navy! I am an Admiral and I ADMIRE servants of the King who memorize the instructions He has given in His Great Book! Over the next few weeks I will have the honor of leading you in such memorization! Sailors—please stand at attention as we read from the King's Great Book! Then we shall learn today's royal memory verse from the Hugga-Wugga™ Paraphrase!

Read Philippians 4:6 from GCENT: Don't worry about anything. Instead, let God know what you are asking for in prayer. Tell Him all about what you want. And, be thankful.

Teach the Hugga-Wugga™ paraphrase *(Hear the rhythm on the CD)*

"Don't worry about ANYTHING—Just BE THANKFUL!
Don't worry about ANYTHING—Just BE THANKFUL!
Tell Jesus what you want; tell Jesus what you need
Philippians chapter 4 verse 6—Always, always be
THANKFUL!"

Memory Verse cont.

WORDS	ACTIONS
"Don't worry about ANYTHING	*Both hands to temples and shake head*
Just BE THANKFUL!	*Hand over hand under chin; look up thankfully*
Don't worry about ANYTHING	*Both hands to temples and shake head*
Just BE THANKFUL!	*Hand over hand under chin; look up thankfully*
Tell Jesus what you want	*Flip left palm up*
tell Jesus what you need	*Flip right palm up*
Philippians chapter 4 verse 6—	*Bring both palms together at chest, gradually on beat*
Always, always be	*Slap hand under hand on beat*
THANKFUL! Be THANKFUL! Be THANKFUL!"	*Cup hand under hand and rock with exaggerated shoulder movements*

REMEMBER.....
Continue to review memory verses from previous lessons.

LEADER *(After thanking KINGDOM ADMIRAL)* Today we will be learning some important lessons from someone who was **not a sailor, but a shepherd. He was someone we can all admire. His name was David.** Most of you are familiar with the story of David and Goliath, but there are many other exciting stories about David. Throughout his life, one thing remained the same. **David was a worshiper.** He praised the Lord when times were good, and when times were bad. **David tried always to have what we will refer to as an "attitude of gratitude."**

KINGDOM SAILORS *(Enter running, wearing white sailor caps)*
CHEER: "Attitude of Gratitude!"

NOTE: The KINGDOM ADMIRAL could be the leader of the KINGDOM SAILORS. NOTE: Use sailor jig actions with the cheer. Example: right hand over right eye while hopping on right foot; then left...

LEADER *(After thanking KINGDOM SAILORS.)* **David had an attitude of gratitude!** As a young man, David looked after his father's sheep. The Bible tells how David killed a lion and a bear that had tried to attack the sheep. David knew that God was with him, no matter what the circumstances. David had seven brothers, none of whom seemed to like David very much. **But instead of getting bitter at his brothers, David chose**

Memory Verse cont.

to sing while watching the sheep—and that's where he was on one very important day. **Well, here to tell you more about David's life are the King's Traveling Minstrels!**

IDE CLARE Wait a minute, sonny! I declare, you are in such a hurry, aren't you! Before you hear the story from those there minstrel fellas, I declare—you'd best hear it right from the pages of the Good Book!

Hello, children. My name is Ide and my middle name is Clare—so I'm Ide Clare! I want to read today's story direct from the pages of God's Good Book, the Bible. Do you have one of these? Then look along with me in First Samuel 16 verses 7 to 11.

(Ide Clare reads the verses and then talks while exiting.)

There now, you can go on ahead with the minstrel fellas. I just wanted to declare the story from the Good Book. I declare!

Sing a Story Theater: David's Song, Part One: "Anointed to Be King"

Creative Illustration 20 minutes

This is a "Kids In Ministry Opportunity!"

The set: Shine a spotlight or an overhead projector on DAVID, who sits off to one side on a low stool. DAVID has a toy lamb and a slingshot hanging from his back pocket. You may want to have a few children pretend to be DAVID'S lambs.

KING'S TRAVELING MINSTRELS: Three comedian-types dressed up to look as much as possible like medieval musicians. One carries a guitar (or mandolin if at all possible!) and strums it once in a while during the song. They should have as much fun as possible—especially when making their entrances and exits. They have wigs, beards, towels, hats, sunglasses—whatever they can find to dress up like David's brothers. **NOTE:** The song can be spoken or make up your own tune.

DAVID: simply acts out the musical narration. He can echo the lines of the songs sometimes, or interject spontaneous ad-libbed comments.

SAMUEL: dressed like Old Testament prophet and carries a flask (full of water to pour on DAVID's head.)

JESSE: just a voice offstage.

The goal of the next few weeks with this is to make David's life memorable to the children—in a fun yet poignant and powerful way. The MINSTRELS can be quite ridiculous but keep DAVID "real."

continued...

Creative Illustration cont.
"Anointed to Be King"

KING'S TRAVELING MUSICIANS
We're here to tell you all a story
About a mighty man *(Oooh…)*
Who started off real little
A shepherd with some lambs *(Baa-Baa)*

DAVID enters and strokes the lamb(s) fondly and dreamily.

KING'S TRAVELING MUSICIANS
When God looks down at people
He sees what no one sees
And when God looked at that shepherd *(Sheep say "Baa-Baa.")*
He could see a king.

So God said to His prophet
"Samuel, do this for Me—
Go anoint the son of Jesse
For I will make him king!"

SAMUEL walks around in a circle like he is traveling. Each time he meets one of Jesse's seven sons, he lifts the flask, ready to pour it if God gives the okay.

SON #1:
FIRST MINSTREL steps forward, acting big and strong.
Hi there! I'm Jesse's son; go ahead, anoint me.

(SAMUEL looks up to check with God, then shakes his head.) Nuh-uh.

SON #2:
SAMUEL walks a bit farther. SECOND MINSTREL steps forward, acting handsome.
Hi there! I'm Jesse's son! Anoint me!

(SAMUEL looks up to check with God, then shakes his head.) Nuh-uh.

SON #3:
SAMUEL walks a bit farther. THIRD MINSTREL steps forward, acting intelligent.
Hi there! I'm Jesse's son! Anoint me!

(SAMUEL looks up to check with God, then shakes his head.) Nuh-uh.

SON #4:
SAMUEL walks a bit farther. FIRST MINSTREL steps forward, acting rich and famous.
Hi there! I'm Jesse's son; go ahead, anoint me.

(SAMUEL looks up to check with God, then shakes his head.) Nuh-uh.

continued

Creative Illustration cont.
"Anointed to Be King"

SON #5:
SAMUEL walks a bit farther. SECOND MINSTREL steps forward, acting like a rock star.
Hi there! I'm Jesse's son! Anoint me!

(SAMUEL looks up to check with God, then shakes his head.) Nuh-uh.

SON #6:
SAMUEL walks a bit farther. THIRD MINSTREL steps forward, acting like a skateboarder.
Hi there! I'm Jesse's son! Anoint me!

(SAMUEL looks up to check with God, then shakes his head.) Nuh-uh.

SON #7:
SAMUEL walks a bit farther. FIRST MINSTREL steps forward, acting like bubble-blowing brat.
Hi there! I'm Jesse's son! Anoint me!

(SAMUEL looks up to check with God, then shakes his head.) Nuh-uh.

SAMUEL scratches his head and uses his fingers to count up to seven; then looks up and talks to God.

Let's see now, I'm supposed to anoint Jesse's son as king. I've seen seven sons and they all looked pretty good to me—but not one of them is the one God wants! Hey, Jesse! Do you have any more sons around anywhere?

JESSE calls from off stage

Yeah, I have one more—DAVID. He's the youngest of them all and he's just looking after sheep. I'm sure he's not the one you're looking for, but—Hey, DAVID—go and see SAMUEL for a minute, will ya?

DAVID, still holding the lamb(s) shyly stands before SAMUEL.

(SAMUEL looks up to check with God, then nods his head in amazement.) You're kidding?! Okay, it's up to You, Lord.

SAMUEL dumps the flask of water on DAVID's head, and says with great authority, "You shall be king over God's people!"

KING'S TRAVELING MUSICIANS
Well, everyone who heard it
Was very much surprised *(Loud gasp and body language!)*
They never thought that God would pick
Such a little guy...

So now you've heard our story
About a mighty man (Oooh...)
Who started off real little
A shepherd with some lambs *(Baa-Baa)*

continued

Creative Illustration cont.
"Anointed to Be King"

DAVID returns to stage area and strokes the lamb(s) fondly and dreamily.

KING'S TRAVELING MUSICIANS
How God made him a king is
Quite amazing
We'll tell more of the story
When we come back——next week!

 LEADER *(After thanking KING'S MUSICIANS)* **Throughout the Bible, David was some-one who had an ATTITUDE OF GRATITUDE!** He didn't become king for many years, but he trusted God all that time. He talked to God in his Secret Place and kept an attitude of gratitude, no matter what! **Now it is time for Part One of** *In Search of Wanderer*.

Creative Illustration 20 minutes

ADVENTURES IN THE KINGDOM™
In Search of Wanderer Part One
"Learning an Attitude of Gratitude"

PICTURE #1: "Seeker's Family"
Seeker looked again at the photograph of his family. Why couldn't things have stayed the way they were in that picture? Why did his dad have to go away?

Seeker's father's name was Wanderer. Wanderer used to live in the Kingdom…he used to live at home…but not anymore. Seeker wasn't sure what had happened, he just knew that he REALLY missed his dad. With a deep sigh, Seeker tucked the picture back into his shirt pocket and kept walking toward Royal Harbor.

PICTURE #2: "Daring"
Doodle and Do's brother, Daring, was a royal officer in the King's service on the sea. Daring used to be gone for months at a time, but now he lived in Royal Harbor and only went sailing when the King sent him out on special adventures.

PICTURE # 3: "Royal Harbor"
Daring had served so faithfully that the King had given him his very own ship, *The Adventurer*. Now in port at Royal Harbor, the ship had become the favorite meeting place for Seeker and his friends. Once a week after school, they had been getting together aboard Daring's ship, *The Adventurer*, for the Adventure Club meeting.

continued

Creative Illustration cont.
In Search of Wanderer Part One

PICTURE # 4: "Kingdom Kids"
When he reached Royal Harbor, Seeker saw his friends. Giggles, Gladness and Glee were laughing, as usual. Dawdle and Slow were quietly tossing cracker crumbs to the sea gulls. HopeSo, KnowSo and Yes were trying to guess how big the ship was and how fast it could go. Doodle and Do were racing to see who could reach their brother first. Daring was standing on the deck, shouting. "Come aboard, everyone!"

PICTURE # 5: "Seeker and Model Ship"
The children loved going to the Adventure Club meetings. Every week they learned something new about the King and his Kingdom; and every week they went on some kind of adventure. For the past few weeks they had all been working hard on building small wooden ships. Seeker was very proud of his model ship.

PICTURE #6: "Moira"
Seeker's sister, Moira, helped with the weekly meetings. "Adventure Club members overcome obstacles with opposites!" she announced.

The children nodded and saluted. "Overcome obstacles with opposites!"

"You overcome evil with…?" Moira asked.

"Good!" the children shouted together.

"You overcome darkness with…?" "Light!"

"You overcome greed with…?" "Giving!"

"You overcome sadness with…?" "Gladness!"

Everyone laughed and patted Gladness on the back, and then they said the Adventure Club cheer: "The Attitude of Gratitude."

PICTURE #7: "Doodle and Do's Sailor Jig"

SAY THE **"Attitude of Gratitude"** CHEER (Have the KINGDOM SAILORS come back to lead it.)

continued

Creative Illustration cont.
"In Search of Wanderer" Part One

PICTURE # 8: "Lantern"

After the cheer, Daring announced, "Each of you will need to carry a lantern with you on today's adventure. Help yourselves to the ones sitting over there on the wooden crates."

As the children each picked up a lantern they talked excitedly. "Where are we going today?" "It must be some place dark if we need lanterns."

Yes was nervous. "I hope it's not too dark—I get scared sometimes when it's dark!"

Moira put an arm around the younger girl's shoulder and smiled as she held up her lantern. "Just overcome the darkness with…?"

"Light!" Yes laughed.

Everyone followed Daring and Moira over the gangplank and back onto the shore. "Wh-wh-where are we going?" asked Dawdle.

Daring smiled at Dawdle. "Caves," he responded, in a low mysterious voice.

"Caves?!" the children echoed.

Daring nodded. "Caves."

PICTURE #3: "Royal Harbor"

Between Royal Harbor and the Castle of Joy and Peace was an underground passageway with a maze of tunnels and caves. Daring had spent many childhood days exploring these. Today he led Moira and the children to a steep cliff at the edge of Royal Harbor, where an entrance to the passageway was hidden behind some trees and bushes. When they reached the entrance, the children were very happy to find someone waiting to meet them…

PICTURE #9: "King"

"King! Hi!" Giggles, Gladness and Glee reached him first, and laughed as the King picked each of them up and twirled them in the air. The others all crowded around for a group hug.

"Your Majesty!" Daring said, bowing.

The King reached out and gave Daring a big hug. Then the King opened the door to the passageway and smiled one of his mysterious smiles. "Shall we?" he asked, and everyone followed the King through the entrance.

continued

Creative Illustration cont.
"In Search of Wanderer" Part One

"S-S-Sure is d-d-dark in here!" called Slow as she and the others lit their lanterns.

Glee laughed and held her lantern high, "You overcome darkness with…?"

"Light!" the others responded.

Yes reached out to the King. "And you overcome fear of the dark by holding the King's hand!"

LEADER And what was inside the cave? We will find out—next week!

Secret Place Time
20 minutes

Play "I'm Loved by God" in the background.

Begin by asking a few children to come up and lead in thankful prayers—not asking King Jesus for anything, just thanking him and praising Him.

Have paper to write THANK-YOU notes and pencils ready for the children. Ask them to kneel in front of their chairs and write THANK-YOU notes to King Jesus, listing at least six things they are thankful for.

Suggestion: *if they want to do so, the children can read their THANK-YOU notes aloud during Small Groups, then put them into their ships.*

Lead in a closing prayer and dismiss to Small Group time. As the children go to their groups, lead in today's "Attitude of Gratitude" Cheer.

Small Group Time

Small Group
20 minutes

GOD'S WORD

Look up these verses and discuss what they mean in the lives of the children this week.

TODAY'S MEMORY VERSE: Philippians 4:6 - *Don't worry about anything; just be thankful.*

Philippians 4:4-7 - *Be thankful and experience God's peace that passes all understanding.*
Psalm 100 - *Be thankful!*
Matthew 5:12 - *Be thankful when people mistreat you!*
1 Peter 1:6 - *Be thankful when life is hard!*
1 Thessalonians 5:16-18 - *Be thankful all the time and in every situation.*
Hebrews 12:2 - *Jesus endured the cross for the joy that was set before Him.*

TALK ABOUT IT TIME
Discuss the following points from today's story:

- **What does it mean to have an "attitude of gratitude?"**

- **How can you "overcome obstacles with opposites?"**

- **How did David do these two things?**

SOMEONE IN THE BIBLE WHO HAD AN ATTITUDE OF GRATITUDE
Acts 16:25 - Paul and Silas sang praises in prison

TOGETHER IN THE SECRET PLACE
(Not many adult prayers, please—let the children pray!)
Sit in a circle. Have the children pray for the child to their right, asking God to help them be thankful, and to have an attitude of gratitude.

                     © 2003 Dian Layton

DOOR HANGER

Duplicate for the children to cut out and take home. Encourage them to hang up this week's door hanger on their bedroom doorknob when they are spending time with King Jesus in the SECRET PLACE.

Shh! I'm with King Jesus in the Secret Place

MEMORY VERSES:
Philippians 4:6
(Hugga Wugga™ Paraphrase)

"Don't worry about ANYTHING—
Just BE THANKFUL!
Don't worry about ANYTHING—
Just BE THANKFUL!
Tell Jesus what you want; tell Jesus what you need
Philippians chapter 4 verse 6—
Always, always be THANKFUL!
Be THANKFUL! Be THANKFUL!"

Seeker's SECRET PLACE

Week #7:
"Run to the King"

MEMORY VERSES:
Psalms 61 and 62
(Hugga Wugga™ Paraphrase)

"I love reading Psalms 61 and 62
When I'm in trouble, I know what to do!
I run to the Rock and I pour out my heart
I do run, run, run; I do run, run
I do run, run, run; I do run, run—to the Rock!"

Secret Sources of Power Quotes

Page 16 - From *Secret Sources of Power*

No one was more dedicated to do the will of God than His Son Jesus. Yet, even though the whole world was lost in darkness, the Bible tells us that Jesus "came apart to rest" or went away from the crowds to be alone for a time. We need to follow His example, especially when a problem or situation threatens to consume our lives.

Pages 17-18 - From *Secret Sources of Power*

God's Word says you can take care of that by unloading or flinging off that weight. If it's a sin, repent of it. If it is a weight or care you have brought on yourself, lay it aside. Are you overloaded with the unrealistic expectations of others? Unload them before you become a slave in the "Kingdom of They-dom." The bottom line is that "the government is on His shoulder," not the shoulders of your critics or would-be slave drivers. Please God before you please man.

WEEK #7: "Run to the King"

Leader's "PRAYERparation"

Please take time to thoroughly read this lesson, as well as the front pages of this curriculum, well in advance of your teaching time.

Run to the King

Where do you run when you are worried or upset? Do you run to the refrigerator? To some kind of addictive substance? To the mall? What about the children in your church—where do they run when they need comfort in times of trouble? King Jesus wants us to run to Him.

One deep area of pain and trouble in the lives of children is divorce. In the story, *In Search of Wanderer*, the fact that Seeker's father left his family may trigger pain within some of the children in your meeting. King Jesus wants to touch their hearts, just like the King touches Seeker's heart in today's story.

Over the past weeks, we have talked about giving our burdens over to the Lord. It is quite likely that some of the children in your meetings listened, but did not really understand; or they have may not been ready to really open their hearts and let out the pain.

There are children in your church who really, really hurt inside. Only God knows what goes on in their homes, and what pain they have endured or have been touched by. Even children from strong Christian homes accumulate painful burdens.

What many children desperately need is a safe place where they can run into the arms of Papa God and unload their heavy burdens. They need to cry, without having an adult telling them to stop. They need a place where they can lie down on the floor if they want and just "soak" in God's presence—unhurried and unhindered.

Will you supply such a place for them this week?

Foundational Scriptures for This Lesson. *Please Read Them...*

Psalms 55:1-2 - *David was overwhelmed by his troubles.*
Psalms 142:2 - *David poured out his complaint to the Lord and told Him his troubles.*
Psalms 34:18 - *The Lord is close to those who have a broken heart.*
Psalms 147:3; Isaiah 61:1; Luke 4:18 - *There is healing for the brokenhearted.*
Psalms 10:14,18; 82:3; 146:9 - *He is Helper to the fatherless*

Today's Memory Verse:
Psalms 61 and 62 - *When I'm in trouble, I know what to do!*
(These are both Psalms of David)

WEEK #7: "Run to the King"

Leader & Small Group Leaders

PRAY FOR THE CHILDREN *before they come into the room today*, .

This prayer is based on Psalms 61:1-3; 62:6-8 *(NLT)*:

"Oh God, listen to the cries of the children of our church! Hear their prayers! From the ends of our community, they cry to You for help, for their hearts get overwhelmed. Lead them to the towering rock of safety, for You are their safe refuge, a fortress where their enemies cannot reach them. You alone are their rock and their salvation, their fortress where they will not be shaken. Their salvation and their honor come from You alone. You are their refuge, a rock where no enemy can reach them.

Oh, children of our church, trust in Him at all times. Pour out your hearts to Him, for God is your refuge!"

Order of Activities (Suggested)

5 min		**Welcome** **Cheer**: "Attitude of Gratitude" with KINGDOM SAILORS
5 min		**Memory Verse** (with the KINGDOM ADMIRAL) **Song**: "I'm Loved by God"; "More, More, More"; "My Hiding Place"
20 min		**Creative Illustration** "David on the Run"
20 min		**Creative Illustration** Illustrated Story *In Search of Wanderer*, Part Two
20 min		**Secret Place Time**
20 min		**Small Group Time**

To maximize the effectiveness of this lesson, here is a **SUGGESTED LIST** of materials:

- IDE CLARE costume
- KINGDOM SAILORS costume
- KINGDOM ADMIRAL costume
- "David on the Run" costumes and props
- **Basics** - Overhead projector, Transparencies, CD Player, Name tags, Bibles, Small Group Pages, Secret Place Doorknob Verse

---

Welcome
5 minutes

KINGDOM SAILORS *(Enter running, wearing white sailor caps)*
CHEER: "Attitude of Gratitude!"

NOTE: The KINGDOM ADMIRAL could be the leader of the KINGDOM SAILORS.
NOTE: Use sailor jig actions with the cheer. Example: right hand over right eye while hopping on right foot; then left...

Welcome cont.

LEADER *(After thanking the KINGDOM SAILORS and welcoming the children)* Today's lesson is called, **"Run to the King!"** Boys and girls, **where do you run when you are worried or upset?** Some people run to the **refrigerator**, because eating makes them feel better. Some people run to a **cigarette**, or an **alcoholic drink**, or some kind of drug to try to take away their worries. Some children can turn to things like **video games** to try to make their hearts feel better. All of these things might help—for a little while. **But then the pain comes back, even worse than it was before.** Be a GOD CHASER! Run to HIM!

Memory Verse
5 minutes

KINGDOM ADMIRAL comes marching in, wearing a Navy cap.

KINGDOM ADMIRAL "Aye, Aye, mates! I am the KINGDOM ADMIRAL, officer in charge of the King's Royal Navy! I am an Admiral and I ADMIRE servants of the King who memorize the instructions He has given in His Great Book! Over the next few weeks I will have the honor of leading you in such memorization! Sailors—please stand at attention as we read from the King's Great Book! Then we shall learn today's royal memory verse from the Hugga-Wugga™ Paraphrase!

Read Psalms 61:1-3; 62:6-8 from NIV: For the director of music. With stringed instruments. Of David. Hear my cry, O God; listen to my prayer. From the ends of the earth I call to You, I call as my heart grows faint; lead me to the rock that is higher than I. For You have been my refuge, a strong tower against the foe.... He alone is my rock and my salvation; He is my fortress, I will not be shaken. My salvation and my honor depend on God; He is my mighty rock, my refuge. Trust in Him at all times, O people; pour out your hearts to Him, for God is our refuge.

Teach the Hugga-Wugga™ paraphrase *(Hear the rhythm on the CD)*

"I love reading Psalms 61 and 62
When I'm in trouble, I know what to do!
I run to the Rock and I pour out my heart
I do run, run, run; I do run, run
I do run, run, run; I do run, run—to the Rock!"

WORDS	ACTIONS
I love reading Psalms 61 and 62 When I'm in trouble, I know what to do! I run to the Rock and I pour out my heart	*Snap right then left on the beat*
I do run, run, run; I do run, run I do run, run, run; I do run, run—to the Rock!	*Fist over fist right then left on the beat*

Memory Verse cont.

 SONGS: "I'm Loved by God"; "More, More, More"; "He Is My Hiding Place"

REMEMBER.....
Continue to review memory verses from previous lessons.

Sing a Story Theater: David's Song, Part Two: "David on the Run"

This is a "Kids In Ministry Opportunity!"

Creative Illustration 20 minutes

The set: Shine a spotlight or an overhead projector on DAVID, who sits off to one side on a low stool. DAVID has a toy lamb and a slingshot hanging from his back pocket. He also has a pair of scissors.

KING'S TRAVELING MINSTRELS: three *(or more)* comedian-types dressed up this week as rock and roll stars from the 1950s. They carry guitars and should have as much fun as possible, especially when making their entrances and exits. Where specified, they sing the narration. Improvise this and use a familiar '50s tune.

DAVID: simply acts out the musical narration. He can echo the lines of the songs sometimes, or interject spontaneous ad-libbed comments. He sings the line of a song, "I do run, run, run; I do run, run."

KING SAUL: dressed in rich kingly robes and crown. NOTE: *David needs to cut off the corner of this, so you may want to use an older robe, or have a piece ready that looks like David cut it off.*

GOLIATH: dressed as a soldier; looks mean and tough.

CROWD: Have the children be the crowd toward the end of the story—teach them ahead of time to shout the chant, "Saul has killed his thousands; but David his ten thousands!" as in 1 Samuel 18:7.

Remember! The goal of the next few weeks is to make David's life memorable to the children—in a fun yet poignant and powerful way. The MINSTRELS can be quite ridiculous but keep DAVID "real."

MINSTREL #1
Greetings, Young God Chasers! We are the King's traveling minstrels, here to tell you yet another story of David, a champion God Chaser!

MINSTREL #2
You might remember our musical story of last week—when we told you how young David, the shepherd boy, was anointed by the prophet Samuel to be king over all Israel.

David walks in with his stuffed lamb and waves shyly at the children; then exits.

Creative Illustration cont.
"David on the Run"

MINSTREL #3
But there was one problem.
Israel already had a king.
His name was Saul.

KING SAUL enters.

MINSTREL #1
Saul used to be a good king—when he trusted and obeyed God. But not anymore. Now he was so filled up with pride and arrogance and anger and fear...that he didn't have any room inside for God.

King Saul *acts proud, arrogant, and angry.*

MINSTREL #2
Well, Israel's enemies, the Philistines, were at war with Israel. Their commander was a giant named Goliath.

He was big and bad and ugly.

GOLIATH enters. He acts big, bad, and ugly.

MINSTREL #3
And every day Goliath yelled at King Saul and his army.

GOLIATH yells a bunch of mumbled words.

KING SAUL cringes and bites his fingernails nervously.

MINSTREL #1
One day, David came to where the army was to see how his brothers were doing, and he saw Goliath and heard what he was saying.

DAVID enters and watches in dismay as GOLIATH again yells a bunch of mumbled words and KING SAUL cringes and bites his fingernails nervously.

MINSTRELS strum their guitars and sing the next narration...

KING'S MINSTRELS SING:
When big, bad Goliath acted mean and tough
David the shepherd boy said, "Hey! That's enough!"

DAVID echoes, "Hey! That's enough!"

He got out his sling and he picked up a rock
And he ran toward the giant in the power of God.

Creative Illustration cont.
"David on the Run"

DAVID holds up sling and invisible rock then swings the sling around and around in the air and begins running toward GOLIATH.

KING SAUL runs to hide behind one of the children in the front row,

DAVID sings, "I do run, run, run; I do run, run!" He hurls the invisible rock and GOLIATH falls down onto his back. DAVID runs and puts one foot on Goliath's chest and waves his arms triumphantly.

 IDE CLARE Excuse me! I declare before you hear any more from those there minstrel fellas, I declare—you'd best hear it right from the pages of the Good Book!

Hello, children. My name is Ide and my middle name is Clare. I'm Ide Clare and I want to read the REST of today's story direct from the pages of God's Good Book, the Bible. Do you have one of these? Then look along with me in First Samuel 18 verses 6 to 9.

(IDE CLARE reads the verses and then talks while exiting.)

There now, you can go on ahead, minstrel fellas. I just wanted to declare the story from the Good Book. I declare!

King Saul was happy that David killed Goliath; at first, anyway.

KING SAUL comes out from hiding and pats DAVID on the back.

Until he heard the people's praise.

Have the children chant: "Saul has killed his thousands; but David his ten thousands!" (See 1 Samuel 18:7.)

King Saul was in a jealous rage
And he tried to kill poor shepherd, Dave.

KING SAUL throws an invisible javelin at David, who ducks and runs, singing, "I do run, run, run; I do run, run!"

David ran through the desert and he ran through the hills
Away from King Saul, David ran until

He came to a cave and he went in to hide
And while he was there, David got a surprise

David hides behind the podium or something else on the stage.

Shhh!
King Saul came to that very same cave
He sat down for a rest that day

Creative Illustration cont.
"David on the Run"

KING SAUL enters, yawning and rubbing his eyes and sits down with his back to David.

Well, David crept over and clipped off a piece
Of King Saul's robe very sneakily…

DAVID tiptoes over and cuts off a piece of Saul's robe. Holds it up, then sneaks back to his hiding place.

King Saul stood up and left the cave

KING SAUL stands, stretches, and exits.

Then David ran and called his name

DAVID holds up the piece of cloth from Saul's robe and calls, "King Saul! Hello!"

KING SAUL grabs the edge of his robe, realizes in dismay what David did.

David could have killed Saul that day
He would have become king that way.

KING SAUL wipes his brow in relief.

But David didn't take things into his own hands
Instead he trusted God to work out a plan.

DAVID waves at King Saul. KING SAUL exits. DAVID stands front and center.

How God made him a king is quite amazing;
We'll tell more of the story when we come back—next week!

David waves and turns to leave.

 LEADER Wait a minute, King's Minstrels! **Hey, David! Can you please come back here for a minute!** Boys and girls, David was the one who wrote Psalms 61 and 62—he knew how to run to the King! David, I hope you don't mind our Hugga-Wugga™ version! King's Minstrels, you will love this!

DAVID comes back. LEADER (or KING'S ADMIRAL) lead the children in today's memory verse. KING'S MINSTRELS and DAVID really get into it; then exit.

ADVENTURES IN THE KINGDOM™
In Search of Wanderer **Part Two**
"In the Cave"

Creative
Illustration
20 minutes

REVIEW THE STORY

PICTURE #1: "Seeker's Family"
Last week we learned that Seeker's father's name was Wanderer. Wanderer used to live in the Kingdom…he used to live at home…but not anymore.

PICTURE #2: "Daring" and **PICTURE #6: "Moira"**
Doodle and Do's brother, Daring, had a ship. He and Seeker's sister, Moira had weekly Adventure Club meetings on the ship for the children.

PICTURE #5: "Seeker and Model Ship"
The children had been working hard on building small wooden ships. Seeker was very proud of his model ship. Each week, Daring and Moira took the children on some kind of adventure. This week they were going to a cave…

PICTURE #3: "Royal Harbor"
Between Royal Harbor and the Castle of Joy and Peace was an underground passageway with a maze of tunnels and caves. Daring and Moira lead the children to a steep cliff at the edge of Royal Harbor, where an entrance to the passageway was hidden behind some trees and bushes. When they reached the entrance to the cave, the children were very happy to find someone waiting to meet them…

PICTURE #9: "King"
The King…

PICTURE #10: "In the Cave"
The King smiled. "Alright now, everyone, there are hundreds of tunnels that lead off from the main passageway, so follow me and stay close together!" The King led the way through the rocky hall. Daring, Moira, and the children "oohed" and "ahhed" over the beautiful rock formations. Stalactites and stalagmites decorated the tunnel with a golden glow under the light of the lanterns.

After many long moments of walking, the King stooped to enter a low doorway. "Cave," KnowSo whispered knowingly. Yes nodded. She had been walking confidently far down the line, but now hurried to take hold of the King's hand once again.

The King stood in the middle of the cave and everyone looked at him. "I want you to experience something for a few moments," he said.

continued

Creative Illustration cont.
In Search of Wanderer Part Two

"What is it, King?" Seeker asked eagerly.

"Darkness," answered the King.

"Darkness?" Yes echoed, holding more tightly to his hand.

"Darkness," the King repeated. He looked around at the children's faces and asked, "Do you trust me?"

"Yes, we DO!" everyone responded, with Doodle and Do's voices loudest of all.

"Then blow out your lanterns," said the King.

PICTURE #11: "Darkness" *Cover the projector screen with a sheet of paper.*
Everyone blew out their lanterns. Immediately, they were in total darkness. It was darker than any darkness they had ever been in before. Giggles, Gladness and Glee giggled nervously.

"This is how some people live their lives," the King said. "In complete darkness."

"That would be very scary," Yes's voice trembled slightly.

"You know my Kingdom as Joy and Peace," said the King. "It is also the Kingdom of Light. Everyone who really knows me, lives in the Light. But the people who don't know me..."

"Live in Darkness." KnowSo said, finishing the sentence.

"That would be a very sad place to live," Moira said softly. "I never want to live in Darkness!"

"Stay close to me, Moira," said the King, "And you won't live in Darkness. Many years ago, your families lived in the Darkness of Fear."

"My mom told me all about that," said Seeker. "The dragon Fear controlled everyone there!"

"Please don't talk about dragons!" Yes said, clutching tightly to the King's hand.

"DO you think there are more dragons out there, King?" Doodle asked excitedly.

"Many more dragons, Doodle," the King answered. "They rule the Darkness and try to keep people blinded, so they cannot see my light."

PICTURE #12: "King Sitting"
Then the King lit his lantern. The warm glow shone on his face and everyone was relieved, especially Yes.

Moira called out, "You overcome darkness with...?"

"Light!" the children shouted as they all lit their lanterns.

NOTE: Have the children join in saying this.

continued

Creative Illustration cont.
In Search of Wanderer Part Two

"You overcome evil with…?"   "Good!"

"You overcome greed with…?"   "Giving!"

"You overcome sadness with…?"   "Gladness!"

Everyone laughed and patted Gladness on the back again. Glee was looking at the picnic basket. "And you overcome hunger with…FOOD! Can we eat now…please?!"

PICTURE #6: "Moira"
Moira laughed and opened the picnic basket she had been carrying. Seeker helped her pass out food to the others. As everyone munched on sandwiches and cookies, the King spoke, "Too many people spend their lives in the Darkness, going through a maze of endless tunnels and caverns." Then the King looked directly at Moira and Seeker. " Some people spend their lives wandering, never finding their way to Joy and Peace in my Kingdom."

When the King said the word, "wandering," Seeker and Moira caught their breath. "Wandering," Seeker whispered. Moira reached out and gave her brother's hand a quick squeeze.

PICTURE #1: "Seeker's Family"
Seeker touched the pocket where the picture of his family was safely tucked. "Wanderer," he said, looking at Moira.

Moira felt the familiar stab of pain in her heart. She had tried to be strong for Seeker's sake, but the long months without their father had been difficult for Moira. Lately she had been telling herself to just accept the fact that he was gone and get on with her life. She had been trying to overcome the pain by not thinking about it; but it wasn't working very well.

The King sat down beside Seeker and Moira. "Dad is living in Darkness, isn't he, King?" Seeker asked.

The King nodded and Moira said, "Dragons. Are there dragons keeping him in the Darkness, King?"

The King nodded again. "There are dragons, Moira," he said, "but they aren't making your father stay in Darkness. He is choosing to stay there." The King looked deep into Moira's eyes and said, "Living in Darkness, or living in my Kingdom, is a choice that each person must make."

"My heart hurts, King," Seeker said. "It really hurts."

continued

Creative Illustration cont.
In Search of Wanderer Part Two

PICTURE #13: "Hand on Heart"
The King very gently touched Seeker's heart. A deep warmth filled him and Seeker felt his pain get smaller. Tears fell down his cheeks and it felt like the pain in his heart was being washed away. "Thanks, King," he whispered.

Then the King reached out to touch Moira's heart but she stopped him, took hold of both his hands, and said, "It's okay, King. I'm fine."

A look of concern flashed through the King's eyes. "You must come and talk to me about how you really feel, Moira," he said.

Moira nodded. "Okay, King, I'll do that," she said, "Sometime soon… I promise. I'll come and talk to you."

PICTURE #4: "Kingdom Kids"
The children had been watching the King speak to Seeker and Moira. "I HOPE Moira talks to the King about how she is REALLY feeling!" said KnowSo.

"I KNOW that's what she needs to do!" agreed KnowSo.

Yes nodded. "Yes—EVERYONE needs to run to the King and give Him all their cares and worries."

"DO you think Wanderer will ever come home?" Do whispered.

I HOPE so!" said HopeSo.

"I KNOW so!" said KnowSo confidently.

"Yes, yes of course he will!" Yes nodded.

After the group explored a few more tunnels and caves, the King led them out through the passageways, and back toward Royal Harbor. When they reached the entrance, the King waved good-bye and they continued on to the *Adventurer*. The children were anxious to work on their model ships.

PICTURE #14: "Model Ship"
And next week we will find out more about what happens to Seeker's ship and what a ship has to do with a person named Wanderer.

Secret Place Time
20 minutes

Music of "He Is My Hiding Place" softly in background. Keep the lights dim.

LEADER Boys and girls, it's time to go into the Secret Place and talk to King Jesus about what we have heard today. Our lesson was called, "Run to the King." **David ran to the Lord when life wasn't fair and things didn't work out like he thought they should. Seeker turned to the King when he thought about his father, What problems do you have? Will you give them all to King Jesus and let Him touch your heart?**

(Suggestion: Ask the children to lie down on the floor.)

We are going to pray together, and then **I want you to just spend time with King Jesus, letting Him touch your heart.** When the King touched Seeker's heart, **Seeker cried and it felt like the tears were helping wash the pain away.**

Sometimes when people unload their burdens on King Jesus, they feel like crying. **It's good to cry.** I think those kinds of tears are like SPIRIT-MAN taking a shower! Tears help wash away the sadness. So, if that feeling comes to you, don't try to stop the tears. You go ahead and cry. **This is a safe place.** Jesus cares about you and so do we. The lights are dim—no one is watching you. Go ahead and give King Jesus your sadness…and then let Him fill you with all the good things He has for His children.

Remember, **the Holy Spirit is your Teacher, Helper, and Comforter.** Let Him be that to you today. Please pray after me…

King Jesus, *(children echo)* thank You for caring about me. *(children echo)* Thank You for loving me. *(children echo)* Thank You that You want me *(children echo)* to give You all my burdens. *(children echo)* Lord Jesus, *(children echo)* You see right inside my heart *(children echo)* and You know how I really feel. *(children echo)* Today, King Jesus, *(children echo)* (SAY DATE) *(children echo)* I unload. *(children echo)* I give you my sadness and pain. *(children echo)* I give you my fears *(children echo)* and my worries, *(children echo)* and pain and disappointment. *(children echo)* Take them, Lord! *(children echo)* Thanks!

And now, King Jesus, *(children echo)* I ask You to touch my heart. *(children echo)* Take away all sadness *(children echo)* and give me peace. *(children echo)* Amen.

Gently encourage the children to quietly wait in God's Presence. Small Group Leaders should move among the children, praying. Watch for any children who are weeping. What they will need most is someone to just hold them and let them cry. If they want to talk, fine, but otherwise, just hold them and pray very quietly. Let God's voice be the one they hear.

Small Group Time

**Small Group
20 minutes**

Look up these verses and discuss what they mean in the lives of the children this week.

TODAY'S MEMORY VERSES: Psalms 61 and 62 -
When I'm in trouble, I know what to do! (These are both Psalms of David)

Psalm 55:1-2 - *David was overwhelmed by his troubles.*
Psalm 142:2 - *David poured out his complaint to the Lord and told Him his troubles.*
Psalms 34:18 - *The Lord is close to those who have a broken heart.*
Psalms 147:3; Isaiah 61:1; Luke 4:18 - *There is healing for the brokenhearted.*
Psalms 10:14, 18; 82:3; 146:9 - *He is Helper to the fatherless.*

GOD'S WORD

TALK ABOUT IT TIME
Discuss the following points from today's story:

- **David spent a lot of time running. He ran AWAY from King Saul and ran TO the Lord. Why did David cut off the corner of King Saul's robe?** *(David trusted God to take care of Saul; he didn't want to work things out on his own.)*

- **What is Seeker's father's name?** *(Wanderer)*

- **What happened when the King put his hand on Seeker's heart?** *(The pain went away.)*

- **What happened when the King tried to touch Moira's heart?** *(She wouldn't let him.)*

- **Did King Jesus touch YOUR heart today? What happened?**

SOMEONE IN THE BIBLE WHO RAN TO THE KING
2 Kings 23:25 - Young King Josiah turned to the Lord with all his heart.

TOGETHER IN THE SECRET PLACE
(Not many adult prayers, please—let the children pray!)
Pray for any children whose fathers don't live at home. Pray that King Jesus will continue to heal their hearts and look after their families. Pray that all the children will run to the King with their problems; and not run to the refrigerator or a game or any addictive substance to try to find comfort.

DOOR HANGER

Duplicate for the children to cut out and take home. Encourage them to hang up this week's door hanger on their bedroom doorknob when they are spending time with King Jesus in the SECRET PLACE.

Shh! I'm with King Jesus in the Secret Place

MEMORY VERSES:
Psalms 61 and 62
(Hugga Wugga™ Paraphrase)

"I love reading Psalms 61 and 62
When I'm in trouble, I know what to do!
I run to the Rock and I pour out my heart
I do run, run, run; I do run, run
I do run, run, run; I do run, run—to the Rock!"

Seeker's SECRET PLACE

Week #8:
"Give It All to the King and Wait"

MEMORY VERSE:
1 Peter 5:7
(Hugga Wugga™ Paraphrase)

"Casting all my cares upon Him—
Because Jesus cares for me!
Pouring out my heart in prayer—
My burdens are released!
First Peter 5 verse 7—HEY!
Give your cares to Jesus then trust Him and wait!"

Secret Sources of Power Quotes

Page 10 - From *Secret Sources of Power*
What do you do when life shows up and God doesn't? You focus on Him anyway and unload the situation into His care. Peter, Jesus' most impetuous disciple, wrote in his later and more mature years, "[Cast] all your care upon Him, for He cares for you" (1 Pet. 5:7).

Page 16 - From *Secret Sources of Power*
Many times these people will say, "I've asked God to take it away and He just won't." You could tell them the truth and say, "No, God said for *you* to do it. The Scripture says, '…let *us* lay aside every weight' (Heb. 12:1a). The job is in your portfolio, not God's." However, don't be surprised if they reply, "I've tried that. I just can't…." God would not tell us to "lay aside" something if we were not fully capable of doing it. It is not that we *cannot*; it is that we *will not*.

Page 19 - From *Secret Sources of Power*
…the Book still says, "Those who wait on the Lord shall renew their strength" (Is. 40:31a). This is another source of secret power. God only promises to renew the waiters—the people who have learned to lay aside and unload other things so they can wait on Him. Learn to wait on God until He hears and answers you.

WEEK #8: "Give It All to the King and Wait"

Leader's "PRAYERparation"

Please take time to thoroughly read this lesson, as well as the front pages of this curriculum, well in advance of your teaching time.

Give It All to the King and Wait

God's timing...it usually seems to take longer than what we would want. Children need to learn the importance of giving their burdens to King Jesus, and then waiting. God places tremendous value on His children having faith, even though they cannot yet see the results they are waiting for. During the times of waiting and trusting, the Holy Spirit is at work within us, building character. **We must cast our cares upon Jesus and wait...knowing He REALLY cares for us.**

Foundational Scriptures for This Lesson. *Please Read Them...*

Matthew 11:28 - *Come unto Me, all you who carry heavy burdens.*
Isaiah 40:31 - *Wait on the Lord and have renewed strength.*
Isaiah 30:15 - *In quietness and confidence is your strength.*
Luke 1:37 - *Nothing is impossible with God.*
Jeremiah 17:7 - *We trust in the LORD and have made Him our hope and confidence.*
Romans 4:21 - *Be like Abraham and be fully convinced that God is able to do what He promised!*
2 Timothy 1:12 - *God is very able to take care of that which we give to Him.*

Today's Memory Verse:
1 Peter 5:7 - *Cast all your cares on Jesus.*

Order of Activities (Suggested)

10 min — **Memory Verse** (with the KINGDOM ADMIRAL)

15 min — **Creative Illustration**
"David Casts All His Cares"
Cheer: "Attitude of Gratitude" with KINGDOM SAILORS

25 min — **Creative Illustration**
Illustrated Story *In Search of Wanderer* Part Three

20 min — **Secret Place Time**
Songs: "The Holy Spirit Song"; "I'm Loved by God"; "He Is My Hiding Place"; "In the Secret Place"

20 min — **Small Group Time**

To maximize the effectiveness of this lesson, here is a **SUGGESTED LIST** of materials:

• Cut-out paper hearts
• Pencils
• Offering Plate
• KINGDOM SAILOR costume
• KINGDOM ADMIRAL costume
• "David Casts All His Cares" Costumes and props
• **Basics** - Overhead projector, Transparencies, CD Player, Name tags, Bibles, Small Group Pages, Secret Place Doorknob Verse

WEEK #8: "Give It All to the King and Wait"

Leader & Small Group Leaders

PRAY FOR THE CHILDREN before they come into the room today, .

This prayer is based on 1 Peter 5:7 (GCENT), Isaiah 40:31 (NKJV) and Jeremiah 17:7 (NLT):

"King Jesus, please help us, as well as the children, throw all our worries onto You, knowing that You REALLY care for us. Your Word promises that those who wait on You—those who put their faith and trust in You—shall renew their strength. They shall mount up with wings like eagles. They shall run and not be weary. They shall walk and not faint. We are blessed because we trust in You and have made You our hope and confidence. King Jesus, help us to give You all our cares and heavy burdens and then wait—knowing and confidently trusting that You are at work on our behalf. Amen."

Memory Verse
10 minutes

LEADER *(After welcoming the children)* Today's lesson is called, "Give It All to the King and Wait." This is a very important lesson, because many people tend to give it all to the King and then WORRY instead of wait!

KINGDOM ADMIRAL comes marching in, wearing a Navy cap.

KINGDOM ADMIRAL "Aye, Aye, mates! I am the KINGDOM ADMIRAL—officer in charge of the King's Royal Navy! I am an Admiral and I ADMIRE servants of the King who memorize the instructions He has given in His Great Book! Over the next few weeks I will have the honor of leading you in such memorization! Sailors—please stand at attention as we read from the King's Great Book! Then we shall learn today's royal memory verse from the Hugga-Wugga™ Paraphrase!

Read 1 Peter 5:7 from GCENT: Throw all your worries onto God, because He cares for you.
From the NLT: Give all your worries and cares to God, for He cares about what happens to you.

Teach the Hugga-Wugga™ paraphrase *(Hear the rhythm on the CD)*

"Casting all my cares upon Him—
Because Jesus cares for me!
Pouring out my heart in prayer—
My burdens are released!
First Peter 5 verse 7—HEY!
Give your cares to Jesus then trust Him and wait!"

Memory Verse cont.

WORDS	ACTIONS
"Casting all my cares upon Him—	*Hold imaginary fishing pole with both hands and "cast it" up and out toward Heaven*
Because Jesus cares for me!	*Let go of the pole and wave like waving cares good-bye*
Pouring out my heart in prayer—	*With both hands at chest "pour out" your heart as you kneel gradually*
My burdens are released! First Peter 5 verse 7—HEY!	*Pull fists to heart* *Jump up, pulling hands apart as the weight is lifted until at the end both hands are raised, totally free!*
Give your cares to Jesus	*Hold imaginary fishing pole with both hands and "cast it" up and out toward Heaven*
then trust Him and wait!"	*Clasp hands behind head and lean back, relaxed.*

REMEMBER.....
Continue to review memory verses from previous lessons.

Creative Illustration 15 minutes

Sing a Story Theater: David's Song, Part Three: "David Casts All His Cares"

This is a "Kids In Ministry Opportunity!"

DAVID dressed in simple shepherd garb and with a "harp."

REPORTER with microphone and clipboard; wearing a trench coat and hat.

DAVID'S SERVANT dressed simply.

David is playing his harp, *(or whatever you have that can be used),* and leaning against a "tree." He is singing the words of Psalms…

DAVID	I will praise You as long as I live, and in Your name I will lift up my hands. Because You are my help, I sing in the shadow of Your wings. My soul clings to You; Your right hand upholds me. *(Psalms 63:4,7,8 NIV)*
REPORTER	Ladies and gentlemen, we are on site in the wilderness near Israel, and today, we get to meet a king! I am scheduled to do a live interview with King David. He is supposed to be around here somewhere…maybe I'll go

continued

Creative Illustration cont.
"David Casts All His Cares"

over and ask that poor fellow under the tree if he has seen King David... Uh, excuse me...?

DAVID   Yes?

REPORTER   I'm looking for King David. Have you seen him?

DAVID   *(Stands up and reaches out to shake reporter's hand.)* I am King David; at least, that is who God says I am.

REPORTER   *(Shocked, he holds microphone away from David.)* Quit joking around! This is live TV!

DAVID   What is live TV?

REPORTER   Never mind, just tell me where King David is!

DAVID   I told you already—I'm right here!

REPORTER   I don't believe you!

DAVID   *(Smiles)* I know, I know. I find it hard to believe as well; but when it comes to things of God, you must have faith! God told his prophet Samuel to anoint me king of Israel, and he did! And now...I wait.

REPORTER   You wait?!

DAVID   *(Nodding.)* Yes, I wait. I could march into Jerusalem and take over, but I will not do that. I will trust God. His ways are perfect. He has called me to be king, and while I wait for that to happen, I will sing to Him, right here in the wilderness! I will have an attitude of gratitude and be thankful—no matter how things appear to be.

DAVID'S SERVANT suddenly runs in, runs over and picks up David's "harp" and hands it to him.

SERVANT   Master David! Master David! Saul is coming! He is very near and he will find you! He will destroy you, sir! Please, hide!

DAVID smiles as he takes the "harp" and puts his hand on the SERVANT'S shoulder. DAVID and the SERVANT both close their eyes and worship as David sings his response...REPORTER wipes tears from his eyes, obviously moved.

continued

Creative Illustration cont.
"David Casts All His Cares"

DAVID   The Lord is my hiding place; He will protect me from trouble and surround
me with songs of deliverance. *(from Psalms 32:7 NIV)*

My soul finds rest in God alone; my salvation comes from Him. He alone
is my rock and my salvation; He is my fortress, I will never be shaken.
(Psalms 62:1, 2 NIV)

DAVID and his SERVANT exit, still worshiping.

REPORTER   *(Wiping more tears away.)* Well, folks, we've just met with a king; actually,
we have met with TWO kings! *(He looks up to Heaven and smiles; then exits.)*

LEADER   David was someone who knew how to give his burdens to the Lord and
then WAIT. **Do you remember today's memory verse?** Let's stand and say
it together! *(Repeat today's' memory verse.)* **When you "cast" a fishing line,
can you do it halfheartedly?** Let's try! *(Pretend to cast a fishing line halfheartedly.)* It doesn't work! **And it's the same when we cast our cares,
when we throw our cares upon King Jesus—we need to do it with all our
might!** That's what David did.

And David had an attitude of gratitude, no matter what was going on
around him!

KINGDOM SAILORS *(Enter running, wearing white sailor caps)*
CHEER: "Attitude of Gratitude!"

*NOTE: The KINGDOM ADMIRAL could be the leader of the KINGDOM SAILORS. NOTE: Use sailor jig
actions with the cheer. Example: right hand over right eye while hopping on right foot; then left...*

ADVENTURES IN THE KINGDOM™
In Search of Wanderer Part Three
"Broken Places"

**Creative
Illustration
25 minutes**

REVIEW LAST WEEK

PICTURE #10: "In the Cave"
The King took Seeker and his friends into a cave. The King talked about how some people live in Darkness and spend their whole lives wandering.

continued

Creative Illustration cont.
In Search of Wanderer Part Three

PICTURE #1: "Seeker's Family"
Seeker and Moira's father's name was Wanderer. Wanderer used to live in the Kingdom…he used to live at home…but not anymore. Seeker and Moira were very sad.

PICTURE #13: "Hand on Heart"
The King touched Seeker's heart, and Seeker felt his pain get smaller.

PICTURE #3: "Royal Harbor"
The children went back to the *Adventurer* to work on their model ships.

PICTURE # 5: "Seeker and Model Ship"
Seeker hummed the "Attitude of Gratitude" song as he tightened the sails, attached the anchor, and set a miniature wooden steering wheel in place on his boat. Then he took his paintbrush and carefully put the finishing touches on the wooden hull.

Finally, with a happy sigh, Seeker proudly carried the little model ship over to his sister. Moira was impressed. "Seeker! It's wonderful! It looks just like the real *Adventurer*!"

"Do you think so, Moira?" asked Seeker, pleased. "I REALLY worked hard on it! I'm done now. Can I leave?"

"Sure," Moira said, "I'll see you at home!"

PICTURE #15: "Trees and Scenery"
As Seeker walked down the path toward the Village of Peace and Harmony, he thought about the Attitude of Gratitude song. He had sung the words so many times, but had never really thought about what they meant, until now. "Hmm…" Seeker said aloud, "An attitude of gratitude in my heart all the time. I wonder how you can have an attitude of gratitude in your heart all the time? How are you supposed to be thankful all the time? Especially…especially…"

Seeker sat down on a rock near the path and set his model ship beside him. He reached inside his shirt pocket and pulled out the little picture of his family. On one side of the photograph were Moira and his mother, Contentment; on the other side were Seeker and his father…Wanderer.

continued

Creative Illustration cont.
In Search of Wanderer Part Three

PICTURE #1: "Seeker's Family"
Seeker shook his head and held back tears that began to form in his eyes. "How are you supposed to have an attitude of gratitude about something like this?! How are you supposed to be thankful when you haven't seen your dad for a long, long time? He never writes; he doesn't even send you a birthday card! How are you supposed to be glad your dad's name is Wanderer?!"

Seeker angrily stuffed the picture back into his shirt pocket. "I don't feel like going home yet," he said aloud. "I think I'll go and see if my boat will float."

He picked up the model ship, and went to one of his favorite places. It was the stream behind the castle.

PICTURE #16: "Stream"
Seeker had a special spot at the stream where he and the King often went fishing and skipping rocks. The first day when Seeker had begun to really get to know him, the King had brought him here. Seeker pulled his shoes off and rolled up his pant legs, and then, very carefully, set the small wooden boat onto the water. Sure enough—it floated! Up and down it bobbed along, like a real ship out on the open sea. Seeker sat down on the grassy shore beside the stream and watched. "Hmm…I sure wish Dad could see my boat! He always liked making things, too. We sure had some good times together."

PICTURE #17: "Clouds"
Seeker lay down on the grass and rolled over onto his back. White puffy clouds moved slowly across the sky above him. Seeker liked to watch clouds, and think about what each fluffy shape reminded him of. Today many of the clouds were in the shapes of animals. Seeker thought about the wooden carvings on his bedroom shelf that his dad had made for him. There were dozens of little animals and all sizes of castles and miniature wooden soldiers; but Seeker's favorite carving was one of him and his dad running together across a hill. Seeker's eyes filled with tears and he shut them tightly. "Dad," he whispered. "Dad, I miss you so much! Will you ever come home? Will I ever get to see you again?"

Seeker opened his eyes and blinked away the tears so that he could see. The clouds still moved slowly overhead. He looked at one especially big fluffy cloud. It looked like a ship…

PICTURE #18: "Cloud Ship"
A ship!

On no! Seeker had been thinking so much about his father that he had forgotten to watch his model ship! He jumped to his feet and ran along the shore, desperately looking at the water. A short way downstream he saw the little boat. There it was—smashed against some rocks.

continued

Creative Illustration cont.
In Search of Wanderer Part Three

PICTURE #19: "Seeker and the Broken Ship"
Seeker hurried into the water and picked up the broken pieces. "My boat! My boat! I worked so hard; and now it's wrecked!" The tears he had been holding back wouldn't stay inside any longer. "My boat! My boat!" he cried.

Then Seeker heard someone whistling. Oh, no! He didn't want anyone to know he had been crying, and he didn't want to have to explain why. Using his shirt sleeve to wipe his nose, Seeker blinked hard and got ready to face whoever was coming. The whistling grew louder. Seeker took a deep breath and looked down the shore.

It was the King.

PICTURE # 20: "King at the Stream"
There he stood on the banks of the stream, looking at Seeker. The King smiled. It was a very, very gentle smile, and he kept whistling. The song he was whistling was the "Attitude of Gratitude." All of a sudden Seeker felt angry. He ran toward the King, threw the broken boat on the ground and cried, "Don't you sing that song! It's an awful song! An awful song!"

The King reached out his great arms toward Seeker, but Seeker was filled with such hurt and anger that he pushed the King's arms away and pounded on the King's chest with his fists. The King stood very quietly and just let him do that. Then the tears came again, this time in such a flood that Seeker didn't even try to hold them back.

PICTURE # 21: "King Holding Seeker as He Cries"
With a deep sob, Seeker's fists fell to his sides, and the King very gently took the boy in his arms, held him close, and just let him cry. The King put his hand on Seeker's heart. He had touched Seeker's heart earlier when they were in the cave, but now he seemed to touch pain that was even deeper inside. The King didn't ask Seeker to stop crying; he just held him and waited until Seeker had cried enough tears to wash some of the sadness and anger away.

Finally, Seeker blew his nose on a tissue that the King handed to him and said, "King, I don't understand. How am I supposed to have an attitude of gratitude? How am I supposed to be thankful? Look at my boat!" Seeker picked the pieces up from the ground. "I worked so hard; and now look at it—it's broken! How am I supposed to be thankful about that?"

"You can be thankful, Seeker, because I know how to fix boats."

Seeker was surprised. "You do?!"

The King nodded. "Yes. In fact, if you give me all the pieces and really trust me, I can fix anything that's broken."

"You can?" Seeker whispered. "Okay, King."

continued

Creative Illustration cont.
"In Search of Wanderer" Part Three

PICTURE # 22: "Broken Ship"
Seeker lifted up all the broken pieces of his boat and the King put them carefully into the pocket of his cloak. Then the King put out his big hand, and Seeker put his little hand into the King's big hand, and they walked toward the village. The "Attitude of Gratitude" song began to stir in Seeker's heart, slowly at first, but then stronger and stronger. He whistled with the King all the way to Peace and Harmony.

Would Seeker ever see his father again? Would Wanderer return to the Kingdom? How long would it take for the King to fix Seeker's boat? Next week, we will hear more of the story, "In Search of Wanderer."

Secret Place Time
20 minutes

While the children sing, encourage them to be like David and really praise the Lord, thanking Him and expressing their confident trust in His ability to take good care of them. Linger in God's presence, giving time for the Holy Spirit to minister to the children. Pass out paper hearts and pencils. Have the children find a quiet corner or place in the room. Ask them to write down a sin, fear, or worry that is in their heart. When everyone is ready, fold the heart and hold between praying hands. Lead the children in prayer then have them bring their paper hearts to an offering plate at the front.

LEADER (*Review today's memory verse.*) Boys and girls, **is there something in your life that is broken or hurting?** You need to cast all your cares—throw all your heavy burdens—on King Jesus. He REALLY cares for you! We've talked quite a lot about this during the past weeks. Giving your cares to the Lord isn't a one time thing. **You will need to go into your Secret Place and give Him your burdens on a regular basis.** Otherwise your heart will begin to get full again. Don't let things build up. **As we worship the Lord today, let's go to the King and cast all our cares upon Him.**

SONGS: "The Holy Spirit Song"; "I'm Loved by God"; "He Is My Hiding Place"; "In the Secret Place"

Small Group Time

**Small Group
20 minutes**

Look up these verses and discuss what they mean in the lives of the children this week.

TODAY'S MEMORY VERSE: 1 Peter 5:7 - Cast all your cares on Jesus.

Matthew 11:28 - *Come unto Me, all you who carry heavy burdens.*
Isaiah 40:31 - *Wait on the Lord and have renewed strength.*
Isaiah 30:15 - *In quietness and confidence is your strength.*
Luke 1:37 - *Nothing is impossible with God*
Jeremiah 17:7 - *We trust in the Lord and have made Him our hope and confidence.*
Romans 4:21 - *Be like Abraham and be fully convinced that God is able to do what He promised!*
2 Timothy 1:12 - *God is very able to take care of that which we give to Him.*

TALK ABOUT IT TIME
Discuss the following points from today's story:

- **When you give your burdens to King Jesus, does that mean He fixes everything right away?**

- **It took many years for David to actually become King. Why do you think that God made him wait?**

- **The King told Seeker he could have an attitude of gratitude even though his model ship was broken. Why?** *(Because the King can fix anything that's been broken.)*

SOMEONE IN THE BIBLE WHO WAITED
Romans 4:18-21 - Abraham waited and waited and waited and never gave up hope. He confidently trusted that God was able and faithful to DO what He said He would do!

TOGETHER IN THE SECRET PLACE
(Not many adult prayers, please—let the children pray!)
Have a big cut-out paper heart. Have the children write the names of people they feel have burdens. then have everyone put their hands on their heart and pray.

DOOR HANGER

Duplicate for the children to cut out and take home. Encourage them to hang up this week's door hanger on their bedroom doorknob when they are spending time with King Jesus in the SECRET PLACE.

Shh! I'm with King Jesus in the Secret Place

MEMORY VERSE:
1 Peter 5:7
(Hugga Wugga™ Paraphrase)

"Casting all my cares upon Him—
Because Jesus cares for me!
Pouring out my heart in prayer—
My burdens are released!
First Peter 5 verse 7—HEY!
Give your cares to Jesus then trust Him and wait!"

Week #9:
"Prayer in the Secret Place"
Bearing Others' Burdens for the King

MEMORY VERSES:
Romans 8:26-27
(Hugga Wugga™ Paraphrase)

"Romans chapter 8:26 and 27
I will pray with the Holy Spirit!
The Holy Spirit will help me when I PR-AY
The Holy Spirit knows just what to say!"

Secret Sources of Power Quotes

Pages 8-10 - From *Secret Sources of Power*

David found himself in that proverbial spot "between a rock and a hard place" the day he returned to Ziklag with his fighting men to find their homes in flames and every single member of their families gone. His men talked of killing David. The crops and animals were gone, their homes were nothing but burning embers, wives and children were gone, and no one knew who took them nor where they went. The missing family members could be dead for all they knew.

David didn't have a nervous breakdown or take on the unnecessary weight of personal guilt over something he didn't cause and couldn't change. He said, "Give me the prayer shawl. Bring me that old ephod." He got under that prayer shawl and said to himself, "I've got to talk to God!" Can you imagine how that looked to his fighting men? In the midst of absolute chaos and emotional ruin, this man just shut down everything and went to prayer....

When we talk about the power of unloading, we also need to realize there are burdens we are *supposed to bear* as part of our responsibilities in the family of God. The Bible tells us to *"bear **one another's** burdens..."*

Page 28 - From *Secret Sources of Power*

The "burden" of the Lord can be a divine assignment for us to accomplish, a spiritual weight we are to bear in prayer until it is accomplished (Daniel bore the burden of his nation on his heart and prayed until he heard a word from God)....

WEEK #9: "Prayer in the Secret Place"

Leader's "PRAYERparation"

Please take time to thoroughly read this lesson, as well as the front pages of this curriculum, well in advance of your teaching time.

Prayer in the Secret Place

Children have an innate desire to pray. First Corinthians 14:15 tells us to pray in the Spirit and with our understanding. We usually train children to have a prayer list and a standard format they use to pray at bedtime—but do we teach them to pray in the Spirit? **Do the children in your church know what it means to have the Holy Spirit teach them how to pray, and to pray through them?** It is then that prayer becomes an ADVENTURE!!

Foundational Scriptures for This Lesson. *Please Read Them...*

Mark 11:24 - *When you pray, believe!*
Galatians 6:2 - *Bear each other's burdens.*
James 5:16 - *Pray for each other.*
Romans 8:26 - *The Holy Spirit will help us pray.*
Jude 20 - *Pray in/with the Holy Spirit.*
1 Corinthians 14:15 - *Pray with the Spirit and with the understanding.*

Today's Memory Verse:
Romans 8:26-27 - *The Holy Spirit helps us pray.*

Order of Activities (Suggested)

20 min **Creative Illustration**
"David in the Secret Place"

15 min **Memory Verse**
(with the KINGDOM ADMIRAL)
Songs: "The Holy Spirit Song";
"In the Secret Place"

25 min **Creative Illustration**
Illustrated Story *In Search of Wanderer*
Part Four

10 min **Secret Place Time**

20 min **Small Group Time**

To maximize the effectiveness of this lesson, here is a **SUGGESTED LIST** of materials:

• KINGDOM ADMIRAL Costume
• "David in the Secret Place" Costumes and props
• **Basics** - Overhead projector, Transparencies, CD Player, Name tags, Bibles, Small Group Pages, Secret Place Doorknob Verse

WEEK #9: "Prayer in the Secret Place"

Leader & Small Group Leaders
PRAY FOR THE CHILDREN before they come into the room today, .
This prayer is based on Romans 8:26 *(God Chasers Extreme New Testament)*:

"King Jesus, You have instructed us to bear each other's burdens, and to pray for each other. We don't know how we should pray, but the Spirit helps our weakness. He personally talks to God for us with feelings which our language cannot express. Today, as we lead the children into a time of prayer and intercession in the Secret Place, we ask You like the disciples asked you: Lord, teach us to pray. We open ourselves up to You, Holy Spirit, to pray through us…even in ways that human words cannot express. Amen."

Creative Illustration 20 minutes

Sing a Story Theater: David's Song, Part Four: "David in the Secret Place"

This is a "Kids In Ministry Opportunity!"

LEADER *(After welcoming the children)* Today we are going to learn about **prayer in the SECRET PLACE**, and to begin our lesson, please welcome the KING'S MINSTRELS!

KING'S COUNTRY FOLK MINSTRELS: three or more comedian-types this week are dressed up as "poor country folks" who speak with an exaggerated drawl. They have musical instruments which could include: guitars, banjos, jars of seeds to shake, jugs to blow in, washboards, and/or kazoos.

DAVID: simply acts out the musical narration. He can echo the lines of the songs sometimes, or interject spontaneous ad-libbed comments.

DAVID'S MEN: as many as you want. They are dressed like Bible characters and ride stick horses. *(The stick horses could simply be wooden poles with balloons attached to the top with eyes drawn on for the heads of the horses.)*

Remember! *The goal of the next few weeks is to make David's life memorable to the children—in a fun yet poignant and powerful way. The MINSTRELS can be quite ridiculous but keep DAVID "real."*

COUNTRY FOLK MINSTREL #1
Howdy, Young God Chasers! We're the King's traveling country folk minstrels, here to tell you yet another story of David, a champion God Chaser!

COUNTRY FOLK MINSTREL #2
You all have been hearin' about David. The prophet Samuel anointed David to be king of Israel…but David didn't get to be king right away.

continued

Creative Illustration cont.
"David in the Secret Place"

COUNTRY FOLK MINSTREL #3
No siree, he didn't! He spent a mighty long time running and hidin' from Saul—you know, that thare fella who was already king.

COUNTRY FOLK MINSTREL #1
Well, today, we want to tell you all a story of something that happened when David was waiting to be king. Are ya ready, fellers? Let's tell the story!

COUNTRY FOLK MINSTRELS grab their instruments, clear their throats dramatically and begin to sing the following words to a familiar country tune of your choice. **Suggestion**: *Sing to the tune of the Beverly Hillbillies theme song.*

MUSICAL NARRATION	ACTIONS
Well, friends gather 'round and hear a story today About when David showed us how to pray He and his men came home one day	*DAVID and his MEN enter, riding stick horses.*
And much to their surprise Their wives had gone away— Taken away, that is Their wives and kids were gone! Stolen!	*DAVID and his MEN search for their wives and kids frantically.*
Well David and his men wept out loud; Yes, they wept very, VERY loud. Their families had been stolen and their homes had been burned down— And, David's men said, "This is all your fault!" "No. it isn't!" "Yes, it is!" "No, it isn't!"	*DAVID and his MEN cry.* *DAVID and his MEN cry VERY LOUD.* *They all get off their stick horses, setting them against the wall.* *DAVID'S MEN point at DAVID and say, "This is all your fault!"* *DAVID: "No. it isn't!"* *MEN: "Yes, it is!"* *DAVID: "No, it isn't!"*
Well, David's men were really upset And they cried out with angry threats "Let's throw stones at David, yes! It's his fault that we are in this mess!"	*DAVID'S MEN look very angry and upset.* *"Let's throw stones at David, yes! It's his fault that we are in this mess!"*

continued

Creative Illustration cont.
"David in the Secret Place"

"Get David!

Get David!

Get David!"

Well, David knew that when life gets tough

When it feels like there's just too much

When you're ready to cry, "Stop, enough!"—

That's the time to cry out unto God.

Jehovah, that is.

King of the Universe!

Mighty, powerful Lord of all!

"Get David!

Get David!

Get David!"

DAVID'S MEN freeze.

DAVID paces thoughtfully…then realizes what he must do.

DAVID falls down on his knees and cries out to God, "HELP! HELP!"

DAVID prays the following verses from Psalms 61 and 62 with great expression:
Hear my cry, O God; listen to my prayer. From the ends of the earth I call to You, I call as my heart grows faint; lead me to the rock that is higher than I. For You have been my refuge, a strong tower against the foe. *(Psalms 61:1-3 NIV)*

Find rest, O my soul, in God alone; my hope comes from Him. He alone is my rock and my salvation; He is my fortress, I will not be shaken. My salvation and my honor depend on God ; He is my mighty rock, my refuge. Trust in Him at all times, O people; pour out your hearts to Him, for God is our refuge. *(Psalms 62:5-8 NIV)*

NON-MUSICAL NARRATION

COUNTRY FOLK MINSTREL #1
Well, doggies! That David was some kind of man!

COUNTRY FOLK MINSTREL #2
That's for sure! Some folks run to drugs or alcohol or something else to try to make them feel better when life gets hard!

COUNTRY FOLK MINSTREL #3
Some folks run to the refrigerator—'cause EATIN' makes them feel better!

COUNTRY FOLK MINSTREL #1
Some folks run to the mall—because SHOPPIN' makes them feel better.

COUNTRY FOLK MINSTREL #2
But David didn't run to someTHING in times of trouble, he ran to someONE! He ran to GOD!

continued

Creative Illustration cont.
"David in the Secret Place"

COUNTRY FOLK MINSTREL #3
Yep, he did! And looky here in the Bible *(holds open Bible)*. It says here in First Samuel chapter 30 verse 6, that "David encouraged himself in the Lord!"

COUNTRY FOLK MINSTREL #1
Yep, and it goes on to say how David asked God what to do! Sometimes when folks get into a troubled time in life, they run around asking all kinds of PEOPLE what to do—and that's all well, and good—but we need to remember to be like David, and ask GOD for help! Let's tell the rest of the story in another bit of song!

MUSICAL NARRATION	ACTIONS
Well, David asked God what he should do And God, said "David, I am with you!" So David and his men hurried off that day To find what was stolen and get it back again! And God helped them! They DID get everything back! Wives and children and all their stuff!	*DAVID and DAVID'S MEN ride away on their stick horses, intent on getting back what was stolen from them!*
	Voices of DAVID and his MEN in the distance shouting, "Hooray! Hooray! We've gone into the enemy's camp and taken back what was taken from us! Hooray! Hooray!"
Well, friends that's our story for you today About when David showed us how to pray; We hope you remember what you've learned today— In times of trouble, go to the Secret Place! That's what David did. He ran to God when he was in trouble. Y'all do the same as David, hear?! *KING'S COUNTRY FOLK MINSTRELS exit.*	

Memory Verse
15 minutes

KINGDOM ADMIRAL comes marching in, wearing a Navy cap.

KINGDOM ADMIRAL "Aye, Aye, mates! I am the KINGDOM ADMIRAL—officer in charge of the King's Royal Navy! I am an Admiral and I ADMIRE servants of the King who memorize the instructions He has given in His Great Book! Over the next few weeks I will have the honor of leading you in such memorization!. Sailors—please stand at attention as we read from the King's Great Book! Then we shall learn today's royal memory verse from the Hugga-Wugga™ Paraphrase!

Romans 8:26-27 GCENT: We don't know how we should pray, but the Spirit helps our weakness. He personally talks to God for us with feelings which our language cannot express. God searches all men's hearts. He knows what the Spirit is thinking. The Spirit talks to God in behalf of holy people, using the manner which pleases God.

Teach the Hugga-Wugga™ paraphrase *(Hear the rhythm on the CD)*

"Romans chapter 8:26 and 27
I will pray with the Holy Spirit!
The Holy Spirit will help me when I PR-AY
The Holy Spirit knows just what to say!"

WORDS	ACTIONS
"Romans chapter 8:26 and 27	*Slow, exaggerated walk (like you are "roamin'") on the beat*
I will pray with the Holy Spirit!	*Stand still and clasp hands in prayer*
The Holy Spirit will help me when I PR-AY	*With exaggerated shoulder movement—like you are coming under a burden, bring fists to belly then forward in a push*
The Holy Spirit knows just what to say!"	*Tap temple with right hand then point out from lips*

REMEMBER.....
Continue to review memory verses from previous lessons.

🎵 **SONGS: "The Holy Spirit Song"; "In the Secret Place"**

ADVENTURES IN THE KINGDOM™
In Search of Wanderer Part Four
"The Secret Place"

Creative Illustration 25 minutes

REVIEW THE STORY

PICTURE #1: "Seeker's Family"
Seeker and Moira's father's name was Wanderer. Wanderer used to live in the Kingdom… he used to live at home…but not anymore. Seeker and Moira were very sad.

PICTURE #5: "Seeker and Model Ship"
Seeker had made a special model ship at the Adventure Club.

PICTURE #19: "Seeker and the Broken Ship"
He put it in the stream to see if it would float, but began thinking about his father and forgot to watch it. It hit against some rocks and got broken.

PICTURE #21: "King Holding Seeker as He Cries"
Seeker cried to the King about his broken boat, and about his father.

PICTURE #22: "Broken Ship"
The King asked Seeker to give him the broken pieces and to REALLY trust him. The King said he could fix ANYTHING that has been broken.

PICTURE #15: "Trees and Scenery"
As Seeker walked with the King through the forest toward Peace and Harmony, he whistled the "Attitude of Gratitude" song. It sure was great to know the King had Seeker's broken ship safely tucked into his royal robe. When they reached Seeker's house, Moira came out and said, "Seeker, don't go in there—Mom's crying again." She turned to the King, "King, would you talk to our mom? Sometimes she misses Dad so much…and we don't know what to say to her."

The King gave Moira a hug. "Yes, I'll talk to her. That's one reason I walked Seeker home today!" The King knocked softly on the door and then went into the house.

PICTURE #23: "Seeker and Moira on the Doorstep"
Seeker and Moira sat down together on the back step.

"Moira, do you think we'll ever see Dad again?" Seeker asked.

"I don't know, Seeker," Moira replied. "He sure has been gone for a long time. I wish he'd write a letter or something. I really miss him."

"Yeah, me too," Seeker sighed.

Moira looked at her brother for a moment and then spoke carefully. "Seeker…I think it's time

continued

Creative Illustration cont.
In Search of Wanderer Part Three

for you to accept the facts. We might never see Dad again. Seeker, you have to realize that our family is broken."

Seeker sat straight up and looked at his sister with amazement. "What did you say?!"

"I said our family's broken, Seeker," Moira repeated sadly.

"Hooray!" Seeker cheered and jumped to his feet.

Moira stood beside him, confused. "Hooray? What do you mean 'hooray'?"

"I was just talking to the King! He said he could fix anything that's broken! It's a long story, but the King came and found me at the stream—my boat was broken…"

PICTURE # 22: "Broken Ship"
"Your boat was broken?" Moira repeated, shocked. "You mean your model ship? What happened?"

"Never mind right now!" Seeker said quickly, "The important thing is that the King said that he could fix anything that's broken! That means he could fix our family!"

Moira shook her head. "Oh, now, just a minute," she said, "I know that the King is really powerful—but fix our family? I don't know, Seeker. That's pretty hard, even for the King."

PICTURE # 24: "Moira and Seeker"
"No, it's not too hard! If he can fix anything that's broken, then he can fix our family! I know it! Listen, Moira, we've never REALLY asked him! It's like we've just given up on Dad; we haven't REALLY talked to the King about him!"

Moira was thoughtful. "You're right," she said. "We've never REALLY asked…"

"I have an idea!" Seeker said, "We could go to the Secret Place—you and I together—to the Secret Place every day and REALLY ask the King to bring Dad home!"

Moira smiled her agreement. "Okay, Seeker! It's certainly worth a try!"

The Secret Place is a special place where people can go and talk to the King. They don't always see him, but he is always there. Seeker had his very own Secret Place in one of the castle towers, and he and Moira began meeting there every day.

They went the first day, but they didn't see the King. Second day—no King. Third day, fourth day, fifth day, sixth day…still no King. Finally, on the seventh day, they decided to go to the Secret Place instead of eating lunch.

Let's count to 7 and go into the Secret Place right now…with Seeker and Moira! 1-2-3-4-5-6-7— HERE WE ARE!

continued

Creative Illustration cont.
In Search of Wanderer Part Four

PICTURE # 9: "King"
When they arrived, the door was open and the King was waiting for them…

"I had to make sure you really wanted this," he said, "because it is not going to be easy."

PICTURE #25: "Window of the Secret Place"
The King led Seeker and Moira to the window of the Secret Place and opened the golden shutters. To Seeker and Moira's surprise, although it was lunchtime, through that window they saw a beautiful night sky.

PICTURE #26: "Stars"
Thousands of twinkling stars shone in the darkness. The King pointed, "Do you see those stars? I made them! And I call each one by name!"

Seeker and Moira looked up at the King with awe. "Wow!" they said together.

Then they looked again through the window of the Secret Place, and instead of the night sky, now they saw a stormy ocean.

PICTURE #27: "Stormy Ocean"
Lightning and thunder filled the scene, and powerful waves came crashing against the window of the Secret Place. Moira and Seeker hid behind the King so they wouldn't get wet.

The King lifted his hand and spoke to the storm. "Peace—be still," he said. And the winds and the waves went calm.

Seeker and Moira again looked up at the King with awe. "Wow!"

PICTURE #28: "Darkness"
The next scene they saw through the window was a dark village. It seemed very sad and empty, and a lonely wind echoed through the streets. Seeker and Moira shivered. As they continued to peer through the dim light, they saw an old building that looked like a store. The sign above the front door was faded, and all of the windows were boarded shut.

PICTURE #29: "Lantern"
They looked more closely, and were able to see inside the store. It was filled with piles of lumber and tools, and stacks of books and papers. Everything was covered in a blanket of dust and cobwebs. On a table in the middle of the room, the low flicker of a lantern was struggling to

Creative Illustration cont.
In Search of Wanderer *Part Four*

fight off the Darkness.

And then, Seeker and Moira saw something else.

PICTURE #30: "Wanderer on Chair"

There, sitting on a chair, with chains around his body and his eyes half closed, was a man. His beard and hair had not been trimmed for a very long time, and at first Moira and Seeker didn't recognize him. Then Seeker gasped, "Dad! That's Dad!"

"Dad?" Moira echoed, "No, that can't be Dad; he doesn't have a beard…Wait a minute, Seeker, you're right. That is Dad! But he looks so awful!"

They watched Wanderer for a moment, shocked at his appearance. Then Seeker pointed and cried, "Look! Dragons!"

PICTURE #31: "Dragons!"

Two incredibly ugly dragons snarled as they came to stand by Wanderer. The dragons laughed viciously as they pulled the chains tighter, but Wanderer didn't seem to notice. He was almost asleep…

Seeker had learned about fighting dragons. When he saw those awful creatures beside his father, courage filled his heart! He would come against the dragons in the name of the King! Seeker began to roll up his sleeves when he felt a gentle hand on his shoulder. "No, Seeker," said the King. "Not this time. Your father likes those dragons."

PICTURE #32: "Through the Window"

"He likes those dragons?!" echoed Seeker and Moira together. "What?! How can he like them?!"

"Your father is living in a place called Despair. He never learned to overcome the obstacles; now the obstacles have overcome him…and he likes it that way. To him, it feels like he is in a safe place."

"He could get away if he wanted to," said Moira as she looked closer. "The chains aren't that tight. I guess maybe the dragons just make Dad feel like he can't move."

"How can they do that?" asked Seeker. "Why are those dragons so powerful, King? What are their names, anyway?"

"The dragons are Discouragement and Bitterness," the King explained. "When they first came to your father, they were quite small; but the more he listened to their voices, the stronger they became. Your father lives in Despair…and he wants to stay that way. He has given up. Discouragement and Bitterness have overwhelmed him."

Moira looked up with tearful eyes. "But, King! Can't you make him leave that place?!"

The King shook his head sadly, "No. Not until he really wants me to."

continued

Creative Illustration cont.
In Search of Wanderer Part Four

Moira turned to him in desperation. "King, that's our father! We can't just leave him there! There must be something we can do! Isn't there something we can do, King?!"

The King looked at Seeker and Moira's earnest young faces, and nodded. "Yes. There is something you can do. I want you to continue to meet here every day in the Secret Place; and as you do, those dragons will not be able to lie to your father anymore.

PICTURE #33: "The Great Book"
And, I want you to really believe that your father will read the Great Book. He used to read it. If he would just open it, I would speak to him."

"All right, King! We'll do it!"

Secret Place Time
10 minutes

LEADER Boys and girls, we have learned a lot during the past weeks about casting all our cares upon the Lord and giving all our burdens to King Jesus. But **there are some burdens He WANTS us to carry.**

King Jesus wants us to be burdened and weighed down with a desire to PRAY for other people. This is HIS burden—that people will come to REALLY know Him. He want us to pray for people who do not know the King or who have wandered from His Kingdom.

You have given all your sin, pain, shame and guiltiness; your troubles, fears, worries, and disappointment to King Jesus. You have emptied yourselves of your heavy burdens…now, **will you accept the burden the Lord would give to you—the burden to pray?**

A prayer burden can feel very heavy. You need the Holy Spirit to help you. He will teach you how to pray and He will pray through you—sometimes with groanings that are too deep to express with words. **The Holy Spirit knows exactly the right way to pray; He knows exactly what people need.**

Boys and girls, the Bible tells us to pray with the Holy Spirit and with our own understanding. **We are all quite used to praying with our own understanding. Right now, we are going to spend time praying with the Holy Spirit, asking Him to direct and lead us in prayer.**

Just like in today's story, let's ask the King to open the "Window of the Secret Place" and show us things the way HE sees them. **Let's ask Him WHO HE wants us to pray for, and HOW HE wants us to pray.**

Are you ready? Let's go into the SECRET PLACE! Find an alone place right now in the room and ask King Jesus to show you.

After 5-10 minutes, quietly have the children go to Small Groups where they will pray for whoever the King showed them.

Small Group Time

Look up these verses and discuss
what they mean in the lives of the children this week.

TODAY'S MEMORY VERSE:
Romans 8:26-27 - *The Holy Spirit helps us pray.*
Mark 11:24 - *When you pray, believe!*
Galatians 6:2 - *Bear each other's burdens.*
James 5:16 - *Pray for each other.*
Romans 8:26 - *The Holy Spirit will help us pray.*
Jude 20 - *Pray in/with the Holy Spirit.*
1 Corinthians 14:15 - *Pray with the Spirit and with the understanding.*

TALK ABOUT IT TIME
Discuss the following points from today's story:

- **What is the "Window of the Secret Place"?** *(God showing us how we should pray.)*

- **What does it mean to have a prayer burden?** *(God puts someone on your heart to pray for.)*

- **Have you ever felt a prayer burden? What happened?**

SOMEONE IN THE BIBLE WHO PRAYED IN THE SECRET PLACE
Daniel 10:3,12 - Daniel prayed and fasted for his nation.

TOGETHER IN THE SECRET PLACE
(Not many adult prayers, please—let the children pray!)
Lead the children (OR let them lead you!) in a time of prayer and intercession. **NOTE**: *When children receive a prayer burden, they might respond with loud crying or moaning. Encourage them to yield and allow the Holy Spirit to pray through them with "feelings which our language cannot express." (Romans 8:26 GCENT)*

DOOR HANGER

Duplicate for the children to cut out and take home. Encourage them to hang up this week's door hanger on their bedroom doorknob when they are spending time with King Jesus in the SECRET PLACE.

Shh! I'm with King Jesus in the Secret Place

MEMORY VERSES:
Romans 8:26-27
(Hugga Wugga™ Paraphrase)

"Romans chapter 8:26 and 27
I will pray with the Holy Spirit!
The Holy Spirit will help me when I PR-AY
The Holy Spirit knows just what to say!"

Seeker's SECRET PLACE

Week #10:
"Overcoming Obstacles With Opposites"

MEMORY VERSE:
Romans 12:21
(Hugga Wugga™ Paraphrase)

"Don't be overcome with evil;
But overcome evil with good!!
Romans 12:21 uh-huh, uh-huh;
Romans 12:21 uh-huh!"

Secret Sources of Power Quotes

Pages 42-43 - From *Secret Sources of Power*

I've been wronged. Who hasn't?

Life's dealt me a bad hand. So what? Join the club.

I was lied to. You're not the first one. You won't be the last one. Your Master was lied to. Are you any better than He is?

Those who were supposed to have been my friends forsook me. Join the club. Jesus is president. They all forsook Him and fled.

If you need help, ask God to help you forgive and release those people or circumstances that have hurt you. Ask Him to forgive you for every sin and failure in your life. He is faithful to forgive….

You were forgiven on Calvary, if you will only appropriate God's forgiveness. Do it now and experience the sweet release that comes when the God of Heaven forgives you once and for all.

Page 50 - From *Secret Sources of Power*

We need to forgive whether we feel we have a "right" to be angry or not.

WEEK #10: "Overcoming Obstacles With Opposites"

Leader's "PRAYERparation"

Please take time to thoroughly read this lesson, as well as the front pages of this curriculum, well in advance of your teaching time.

Overcoming Obstacles With Opposites

In today's lesson we will learn where Seeker's father, Wanderer, has been living, and what has been happening to him since his children have been praying for him in the SECRET PLACE. Wanderer never learned to overcome the obstacles in his life; the obstacles overcame him instead. Two dragons named Bitterness and Discouragement have had him under their control as a result. **From today's lesson the children will learn the power of the King's forgiveness, and the importance of applying what they have learned in this curriculum: run to the King in times of trouble; pour out your burdens in the SECRET PLACE; choose to have an attitude of gratitude no matter what your circumstances.**

Foundational Scriptures for This Lesson. *Please Read Them...*

Matthew 5:38-42 - *Turn the other cheek;*
do the opposite of what you feel like doing.
Romans 12:17; 1 Peter 3:9; 1 Thessalonians 5:15 - *Do not repay evil with evil.*
Hebrews 12:15 - *Watch out that no root of bitterness springs up.*
John 14:6 - *There is only one Answer!*
Romans 12:12 - *Don't give up!*
Isaiah 61:1 - *There is healing for broken hearts...*

Today's Memory Verse:
Romans 12:21 - *Overcome evil with good!*

Order of Activities (Suggested)

 15 min   Welcome
Songs: Review
Cheers: "Unloading" with CANDY RAPPERS;
"Attitude of Gratitude" with KINGDOM
SAILORS

 10 min   Memory Verse
(with the KINGDOM ADMIRAL)

 25 min   Creative Illustration
Illustrated Story *In Search of Wanderer*
Part Five
Cheer: "Attitude of Gratitude" with
KINGDOM SAILORS

 20 min   Secret Place Time

 20 min   Small Group Time

To maximize the effectiveness
of this lesson, here is a
SUGGESTED LIST of materials:

• CANDY RAPPERS costumes
• KINGDOM SAILORS costume
• KINGDOM ADMIRAL costume
• SPIRIT MAN booklets
• **Basics** - Overhead projector,
Transparencies, CD Player,
Name tags, Bibles, Small Group Pages,
Secret Place Doorknob Verse

                     © 2003 Dian Layton

WEEK #10: "Overcoming Obstacles With Opposites"

Leader & Small Group Leaders

PRAY FOR THE CHILDREN *before they come into the room today*, .

This prayer is based on Romans 12:17, 21 *(God Chasers Extreme New Testament)*:

"King Jesus, Your ways are so much higher than our ways. What You ask us to do is so often just the opposite of what we would want to do! You said not to let evil defeat us but, instead, to use good to defeat evil. You said to be sure that no one pays back wrong with a wrong. Instead, we are to always try to do good to one another and to everyone. Lord, we need Your HELP! Help us and help the children never to return evil for evil; but to bless people who hurt us! Amen."

Welcome
15 minutes

LEADER *(After welcoming the children)* Today's lesson is called, **"Overcoming Obstacles With Opposites."** We will also do a quick review of all our songs and memory verses in preparation for the up-coming FAMILY ADVENTURE in the sanctuary.

SONGS: Review all songs

CHEERS: Review "Unloading" with the CANDYRAPPERS; "Attitude of Gratitude" with the KINGDOM SAILORS

MEMORY VERSES: Review all memory verses. KINGDOM RUNNER review Weeks # 1-5; KINGDOM ADMIRAL review Weeks # 6-9 *(and then teach Week #10)*

Memory Verse
10 minutes

KINGDOM ADMIRAL

Sailors—please stand at attention as we read from the King's Great Book! Then we shall learn today's royal memory verse from the Hugga-Wugga™ Paraphrase! We will be learning Romans 12:21, but because this part of the King's Great Book is so important to today's lesson, we will begin reading at verse 17.

Romans 12:17-21 GCENT: If someone does wrong to you, don't pay him back with another wrong. Be sure you do what everyone already knows is right. If possible, from your part, live in peace with everybody. Don't avenge yourselves, dear friends. Instead, leave room for God to punish. This is written: "The Lord says, 'Revenge belongs to me—I will pay it back'!" "If your enemy is hungry, feed him. If he is thirsty, give him something to drink. By doing this, you will make him burn up with shame." Don't let evil defeat you. Instead, use good to defeat evil.

Teach the Hugga-Wugga™ paraphrase *(Hear the rhythm on the CD)*

"Don't be overcome with evil;
But overcome evil with good!!
Romans 12:21 uh-huh, uh-huh;
Romans 12:21 uh-huh!"

Memory Verse cont.

WORDS	ACTIONS
"Don't be overcome with evil	*Get pushed back by an invisible wave of evil*
But overcome evil with good!!	*Resolutely push invisible wave away*
Romans 12:21 uh-huh, uh-huh; Romans 12:21 uh-huh"	*Slow, exaggerated walk (like you are "roamin'") on the beat*

REMEMBER.....
Continue to review memory verses from previous lessons.

LEADER *(After thanking the KING'S ADMIRAL)* Now we will hear what has been happening in the Seeker story, and how today's story really teaches us the importance of "Overcoming Opposites With Opposites."

Creative Illustration 25 minutes

ADVENTURES IN THE KINGDOM™
In Search of Wanderer Part Five
"In Search of Wanderer"

REVIEW THE STORY

PICTURE #1: "Seeker's Family"
Seeker and Moira's father's name was Wanderer. Wanderer used to live in the Kingdom... he used to live at home...but not anymore. Seeker and Moira were very sad.

PICTURE #5: "Seeker and Model Ship"
Seeker had made a special model ship at the Adventure Club.

PICTURE #19: "Seeker and the Broken Ship"
He put it in the stream to see if it would float, but began thinking about his father and forgot to watch it. It hit against some rocks and got broken.

PICTURE #21: "King Holding Seeker as He Cries"
Seeker cried to the King about his broken boat, and about his father.

PICTURE #22: "Broken Ship"
The King asked Seeker to give him the broken pieces and to REALLY trust him. The King said he could fix ANYTHING that has been broken.

continued

Creative Illustration cont.
In Search of Wanderer Part Five

PICTURE #32: "Through the Window"

Seeker and Moira went to the SECRET PLACE together to talk to the King about their father. The King showed them, through the Window of the SECRET PLACE, that Wanderer was living on the Island of Despair. He was with two dragons: Discouragement and Bitterness. He had never learned to overcome the obstacles; now the obstacles have overcome him…

PICTURE #9: "King"

Seeker and Moira continued to meet faithfully in the SECRET PLACE, talking to the King about their father. The days and weeks passed. Then, one morning, the King told the children that it was a special day—he and Daring and Moira were going to take them on a real adventure out on the open sea! *(Daring was Doodle and Do's older brother.)*

PICTURE #3: "Royal Harbor"

Everyone packed a lunch and waved good-bye to their friends and families on the shore. The boat left the dock and went out, out, out onto the water. They sailed for a long time. Seeker and his friends took turns steering the ship. They stood on the deck, letting the wind fly through their hair and watching the waves slap the sides of the great tall ship with a gentle rhythm.

PICTURE #7: "Doodle and Do's Sailor Jig"

Doodle and Do led everyone in singing the Attitude of Gratitude song, trying to do their sailor jig while the ship rocked back and forth.

SAY THE CHEER (Have the KINGDOM SAILORS lead it.)

Around noon, after everyone had finished lunch, the King came up from the captain's quarters in the lower part of the ship. "We are on the Sea of Sadness," he said, pulling a knapsack onto his back. "I must leave you for awhile. If a storm should come up while I'm gone, I want you to overcome it with…?"

"Gladness!" the children responded quickly. But they didn't slap Gladness on the back like usual; they were too curious.

"Where are you going, King?" KnowSo wanted to know.

"What are you going to DO?" Doodle asked.

PICTURE #34: "The King's Wink"

The King didn't answer, he just smiled and winked. Then he climbed down the rope ladder on the side of the ship's hull, and into a little rowboat that was tied alongside. Moira, Daring, and the children watched the King row the boat until a fog rolled in across the Sea of Sadness, and the King disappeared from their sight.

continued

Creative Illustration cont.
In Search of Wanderer Part Five

PICTURE #35: "King on the Island"
Through the dense fog, the King rowed to an island. He pulled the boat up onto the shore and tied it securely. Then, glancing around to make sure that no one was watching, the King reached inside the knapsack and pulled out an ordinary-looking peasant cloak. He removed his royal cloak, folded it, and placed it inside the knapsack in the rowboat.

Then the King put the peasant cloak over his royal clothing, and turned toward a path leading through the forest. A rugged sign pointed the way to the Village Despair.

The King smiled one of his most mysterious smiles. He pulled the hood of the peasant cloak up over his head, and stepped onto the shaded path…toward Despair.

Despair is a terrible place where too many people live. It is sad, dark, and very lonely. But in that place, the King heard someone whistling the "Attitude of Gratitude" song! He walked through the streets until he reached the place where the whistling was coming from.

PICTURE #36: "Sign: WANDERER'S WOODWORKING"
There, right in the middle of Despair, was a freshly painted store. The windows were clean and shiny. A brand new sign was hanging above the door: "Wanderer's Woodworking."

The King buttoned his cloak and made sure that his hood was still in place. Then, after pausing for a moment with another of his mysterious smiles, the King walked through the door…

PICTURE #37: "Inside the Store"
The store looked much different than when Seeker and Moira had seen it through the window of the Secret Place. Everything was clean and tidy. The dust and cobwebs were gone, the tools were all neatly in their places, the books and papers were organized, and the Great Book was open on the table near the bright glow of the lantern.

PICTURE #38: "Chained Dragons"
In a far corner the dragons, Discouragement and Bitterness, were gagged and chained! The very chains they had used on Wanderer now covered them! When the dragons saw the King they squirmed in pain and cried, "Mmpphh!" The King smiled again.

PICTURE #39: "Bow and Arrows"
Wanderer was bent over his workbench, busily making some bows and arrows. He looked up, saw the stranger in a cloak, and reached out his hand in greeting, "Good day, sir! My name is Wanderer. And you are….?"

continued

Creative Illustration cont.
"In Search of Wanderer" Part Five

"I am...Answer!" the King said, shaking Wanderer's hand firmly.

"Well, it's good to meet you, Answer! Is there anything I can help you with?"

PICTURE #40: "Wooden Castle"
The King reached toward a shelf beneath the window and picked up a beautifully carved castle. He examined it closely while Wanderer smiled, feeling shy about his craftsmanship. "Very, very nice," said the King.

"Do you like castles, sir?" Wanderer asked.

"Yes, I like castles. And I like this particular one very much."

Wanderer nodded. "As I carved it I was remembering such a castle from my past..."

When Answer appeared to be puzzled, Wanderer explained. "The Kingdom of Joy and Peace, sir. I used to live there. The great King has such a castle."

"Really?" said the King as he set the castle down and picked up an arrow. "Tell me about what you have been working on today."

PICTURE #41: "Bow and Arrow"
Wanderer proudly held up a bow and another arrow. "I make the best bows and arrows in the land, sir. Some of them are heavy and strong; others are light-weight, and all have great accuracy and balance. Each one is made for a special reason—a special purpose!"

"Really?" the King spoke thoughtfully, as he inspected the arrow. "You know, that reminds me of people. Every person is made for a special reason—a special purpose." Answer set the arrow down and turned toward Wanderer.

"What is your special purpose, Wanderer?"

Wanderer was surprised and suddenly felt very embarrassed. "Special purpose? Why...I don't know, sir! I suppose I have searched all my life for my special purpose; but I've never found it."

PICTURE #42: "Open Great Book"
The King walked over to the Great Book, open on the table. The lantern beside it glowed even more brightly as the King approached. "Have you searched here, Wanderer?"

"I used to, sir," replied Wanderer, "and I have been again lately." Wanderer walked across the room and stood beside Answer and the Great Book. "You know, it tells the most amazing story about a King!"

"Really? Tell me about this King."

continued

Creative Illustration cont.
"In Search of Wanderer" Part Five

"Well, it seems that the King loved his people so much that he left his throne, left his Kingdom, and went right down to where they were!"

"Hmm…" said the King softly, "then what happened?"

"He made himself look like one of the people," Wanderer said, "He wore a disguise—so they didn't realize who he was…"

"I see," said the King.

Wanderer picked up the Great Book and continued, "The King did miracles, and told stories about his Kingdom. He explained to the people how much the King loved them—but they didn't understand…"

Wanderer shook his head sadly. "They didn't understand. I was just reading today, how the people turned against him.

PICTURE #43: "Jesus on the Cross"
They took nails and put them into his hands and his feet and they…they killed him!" Wanderer set the Book back on the table, shaking his head in dismay. "They killed Him."

Slowly, the King pushed back the hood of his cloak and spoke softly, "He didn't stay dead, Wanderer."

Wanderer gasped, ""Wh…what…?"

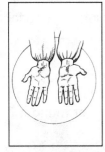

PICTURE #44: "Old Scars"
Then the King held out his hands—revealing two old and faded scars—and Wanderer whispered in amazement, "King! You are the King…and not just the King; you are the real King…You are the King in the Great Book!"

The King nodded and spoke with gentle strength. "The King did not stay dead, Wanderer…and he is still the Answer to everything you have ever searched for."

PICTURE #45: "Wanderer and the King"
Wanderer looked into the eyes of the King, took hold of the wounded hands, and knelt down. "Your Majesty," he said.

And as he knelt, the dragons in the corner grew smaller and smaller and smaller…until they disappeared.

And we will hear the conclusion of the story next week…

continued

© 2003 Dian Layton

Secret Place Time
20 minutes

 (keep the lights dim during this time)

LEADER Boys and girls, we need to really think about today's story. **Do you know anyone who is living in Despair?** It is a terrible place. It is sad, dark, and very lonely.

Do you remember how Wanderer ended up there? He never learned to overcome the obstacles in his life; the obstacles overcame him instead. **The dragons named Bitterness and Discouragement had him under their control as a result.** Despair is not a good place to live. If you ever find yourself there, get out! King Jesus is the Answer. Kneel before Him and any dragons—like Discouragement, Bitterness, Fear, or Greed—that have been trying to hold you captive will lose their power! **The King is stronger than any dragon!**

But **you NEVER have to live in Despair,** and you NEVER have to be held captive by any dragons! **The way to avoid it is to DO what you have been learning in this curriculum! Run to the King in times of trouble; pour out your burdens in the SECRET PLACE; choose to have an attitude of gratitude no matter what your circumstances; and overcome obstacles with opposites.**

Let's go to the SECRET PLACE together right now and talk to the King…

(Pass out little blankets or pieces of cloth for the children to hide under while they talk to the King.)

"Hi, King Jesus. *(children echo)* Thank You so much for today's story. *(children echo)* I never want to live in Despair. *(children echo)* Please help me *(children echo)* to overcome obstacles with opposites. *(children echo)* Help me to run to You in times of trouble. *(children echo)* Help me to pour out my burdens to You in the SECRET PLACE. *(children echo)* Help me to choose to have an attitude of gratitude *(children echo)* no matter what my circumstances are. *(children echo)* Thank You, King Jesus. *(children echo)* Amen."

NOTE: *Also have SPIRIT-MAN booklets available during this time and be prepared to pray with any children who want to ask Jesus into their hearts or make a new commitment to Him.*

After hearing today's story, there may be children who need to or want to respond to the Gospel message.

Small Group Time

Small Group
20 minutes

Look up these verses and discuss what they mean in the lives of the children this week.

TODAY'S MEMORY VERSE: Romans 12:21 - *Overcome evil with good!*

Matthew 5:38-42 - *Turn the other cheek; do the opposite of what you feel like doing.*
Romans 12:17; 1 Peter 3:9; 1 Thessalonians 5:15 - *Do not repay evil with evil.*
Hebrews 12:15 - *Watch out that no root of bitterness springs up.*
John 14:6 - *There is only one Answer!*
Romans 12:12 - *Don't give up!*
Isaiah 61:1 - *There is healing for broken hearts...*

TALK ABOUT IT TIME

Discuss the following points from today's story:

- **What are some ways you can avoid ever living in Despair?** *(Run to the King in times of trouble; pour out your burdens in the Secret Place; choose to have an attitude of gratitude no matter what your circumstances; and overcome obstacles with opposites.)*

SOMEONE IN THE BIBLE WHO OVERCAME OBSTACLES WITH OPPOSITES

Genesis 45:5,7 - Joseph treated his brothers opposite to the way they had treated him. He could have been filled with bitterness and discouragement; but he chose instead to see God's hand in his circumstances. *(Maybe Joseph knew the song, "I'm loved by God"!)*

TOGETHER IN THE SECRET PLACE

(Not many adult prayers, please—let the children pray!)
Ask the King to give you His prayer burden for people who need to be set free from dragons like Bitterness or Discouragement. Spend time praying together for people who live in Despair *(Encourage the children to go into their Secret Place and pray every day for who the King has put on their heart.)*

© 2003 Dian Layton

DOOR HANGER

Duplicate for the children to cut out and take home. Encourage them to hang up this week's door hanger on their bedroom doorknob when they are spending time with King Jesus in the SECRET PLACE.

Shh! I'm with King Jesus in the Secret Place

MEMORY VERSE:
Romans 12:21
(Hugga Wugga™ Paraphrase)

*"Don't be overcome with evil;
But overcome evil with good!!
Romans 12:21 uh-huh, uh-huh;
Romans 12:21 uh-huh!"*

Seeker's SECRET PLACE

Week #11:
"Singing a New Song
Overcome Sadness With Gladness"
Bearing Others' Burdens for the King

Secret Sources of Power Quotes

Page 21 - From *Secret Sources of Power*
When we take our eyes off Him—even at the height of our earthly ministry—we can quickly become over-loaded by a burden that is "easy" when it is borne on a shared yoke with God. When we look away from the Master, as Peter did while walking on the water, we immediately begin to sink into what was solid only seconds earlier.

Pages 10-11 - From *Secret Sources of Power*
Someone might say, "I'm climbing a rough, rough mountain." Be thankful! If it weren't rough, it would be virtually impossible to climb because you can't climb a smooth mountain—there are no outcroppings to hold on to. The very things we think are sent to destroy us are often sent to conform us to Christ's image. They come into our lives to build spiritual strength.

   Tests and trials often come into our lives to help us learn a crucial lesson in our walk with God. How will you ever *know* that "He who is in you is greater than he who is in the world" (1 Jn. 4:4b), if you don't overcome a temptation through the supernatural power of His Spirit within you?

WEEK #11: "Singing a New Song"

Leader's "PRAYERparation"

Please take time to thoroughly read this lesson, as well as the front pages of this curriculum, well in advance of your teaching time.

Singing a New Song

In today's Seeker story, the children are on the ship and drift into the Sea of Sadness. Winds of Weariness blow and the children learn about the power of singing to their sadness and overcoming it with gladness. What a life lesson! Can you lift your voice in the midst of the storm and sing praises? Can the children in your church fellowship? Perhaps today's lesson will help everyone realize **the power there is when God's people choose to sing unto the Lord a new song!**

Foundational Scriptures for This Lesson. *Please Read Them...*

Psalms 32:7 - *He surrounds me with the song of deliverance.*
2 Samuel 22:1-50 - *David sang about God's deliverance.*
Psalms 33:3; 144:9; Isaiah 42:10; Revelation 5:9 - *Sing unto the Lord a NEW SONG.*
Psalms 41:5-9,13 - *David was in misery, yet he chose to sing praises to the Lord.*
Isaiah 61:1; Luke 4:18; Psalms 147:2 - *There is healing for broken hearts.*
1 Corinthians 14:15 - *Sing in the spirit and also with words you understand.*
Zephaniah 3:17 - *The Lord rejoices over us with singing!*

Today's Memory Verse:
Psalms 42 - *Sing to the sadness! (The Psalms are songs!)*

Order of Activities (Suggested)

10 min 	**Welcome**	
	Songs: "I'm Loved by God"; "The Holy Spirit Song";	
10 min	**Memory Verse** (with the KINGDOM ADMIRAL)	
20 min	**Creative Illustration** " David Sings Psalms"	
20 min	**Creative Illustration** Illustrated Story *In Search of Wanderer* Conclusion	
20 min	**Secret Place Time**	
10 min	**Small Group Time**	

To maximize the effectiveness of this lesson, here is a
SUGGESTED LIST of materials:

- IDE CLARE costume
- KINGDOM ADMIRAL costume
- "David Sings Psalms" Costumes and props
- **Basics** - Overhead projector, Transparencies, CD Player, Name tags, Bibles, Small Group Pages, Secret Place Doorknob Verse

  © 2003 Dian Layton

WEEK #11: "Singing a New Song"

Leader & Small Group Leaders
PRAY FOR THE CHILDREN *before they come into the room today,* .

This prayer is based on verses from David's prayer in 2 Samuel 22 and Zephaniah 3:17 *(NIV)*; but please do not be limited to these words! Let the Holy Spirit sing and pray for the children through you today. Pray the following prayer with "free singing."

"Oh, Lord, like David sang to You when You delivered him from the hand of all his enemies and from the hand of Saul, we sing to You on behalf of the children who need Your deliverance! We sing this song to You, Lord:

You are to the children their Rock, their Fortress and their Deliverer; You are their Rock, in whom they take refuge, their Shield and the horn of their salvation. You are their stronghold, their refuge and their Savior—from violent men and situations you save them. When they call to You, LORD, who is worthy of praise, they are saved from their enemies.

Lord, help the children in their times of distress to call to You, oh God! Hear their voices; let their cry come to Your ears. Reach down from on high and take hold of them; draw them out of deep waters. Rescue them from their powerful enemy, from their foes, who were too strong for them. Oh, Lord, You live! Praise be to our Rock! Exalted be God, the Rock, our Savior!

LORD our God, You are with us! You are mighty to save. You take great delight in Your children. You quiet them with Your love; You rejoice over them with singing."

🎵 **SONGS**: "I'm Loved by God"; "The Holy Spirit Song"

Welcome
10 minutes

LEADER *(After welcoming the children)* We are nearly at the end of this curriculum. Next week we will spend time in "PRAYERparation" for our FAMILY ADVENTURE in the sanctuary. We have one more memory verse to learn, one more story of David, and the exciting conclusion to the Seeker story, *In Search of Wanderer.* Today's lesson is called, "**Singing a New Song—Overcome Sadness With Gladness.**"

KINGDOM ADMIRAL comes marching in, wearing a Navy cap.

Memory Verse
10 minutes

KINGDOM ADMIRAL Sailors—please stand at attention as we read from the King's Great Book! Then we shall learn today's royal memory verse from the Hugga-Wugga™ paraphrase! Today we will be learning about the importance of singing to your sadness. Let's read some verses from Psalms 42.

Memory Verse cont.

Have a child read:

Psalms 42:6-8 (NLT) My God! Now I am deeply discouraged, but I will remember Your kindness...I hear the tumult of the raging seas as Your waves and surging tides sweep over me. Through each day the LORD pours His unfailing love upon me, and through each night I sing His songs, praying to God who gives me life.

Psalms 42:11 (NLT) Why am I discouraged? Why so sad? I will put my hope in God! I will praise Him again—my Savior and my God!

Teach the Hugga-Wugga™ Paraphrase *(Hear the rhythm on the CD)*

"I speak to the sadness in my heart—
'Hey, HEART! You believe!'
I'll read some verses from Psalm 42 and
I-WILL-SING!"

WORDS	ACTIONS
"I speak to the sadness in my heart—	*Hands cupped on either side of mouth and look toward heart*
'Hey, HEART! You believe!'	*Hands still cupped, shout toward heart*
I'll read some verses from Psalm 42 and	*With right hand, flip through pages of open Bible lying on left palm*
I— WILL— SING!"	*Resolutely stomp one foot* *Left hand on heart* *Right arm up and out dramatically*

REMEMBER.....
Continue to review memory verses from previous lessons.

Creative Illustration
20 minutes

Sing a Story Theater: David's Song, Part Five: "David Sings Psalms"

This is a "Kids In Ministry Opportunity!"

NOTE - *this is real! Don't make fun here.*

DAVID dressed in royal robes and a crown; still has his "harp."
REPORTER with microphone and clipboard. He speaks as if being filmed on live TV.
DAVID'S SERVANT dressed also in royal robes.

© 2003 Dian Layton

Creative Illustration cont.
"David Sings Psalms"

David is sitting on his throne and playing his harp or whatever you have that can be used. His eyes are closed in worship as he sings the words of Psalms...

DAVID   I waited patiently for the Lord; He turned to me and heard my cry. He lifted me out of the slimy pit, out of the mud and mire; He set my feet on a rock and gave me a firm place to stand. He put a new song in my mouth, a hymn of praise to our God. Many will see and fear and put their trust in the Lord. *(Psalms 40:1-3 NIV)*

REPORTER   Ladies and gentlemen, we are on site again in Israel. Perhaps you tuned in a few weeks ago when we met David out in the wilderness. Time has passed, and today, we get to meet a real, live, authentic king! I am scheduled to do a live interview with King David. I will ask his servant if we can speak to David now...Uh, excuse me...?

SERVANT   *(Whispering)* Yes?

REPORTER   I'm supposed to interview King David. Can you tell him I'm here?

DAVID   *(Stands up and reaches out to shake reporter's hand.)* Hello again, my friend!

REPORTER   Your Majesty! You look so much different than the last time we spoke! But, you are still singing!

DAVID   I love to sing to the Lord! I love to lift my voice in praise to Him and sing new songs to Him!

REPORTER   These songs you sing, they seem to be an important part of your life!

DAVID   *(Laughing)* Most definitely, they are! With my songs, I command my soul to trust in God! With my songs, I sing to my heart and tell it to be strong! I command my heart to believe in the Lord and His goodness!

REPORTER   So, King David, would you say that singing songs has helped you to get where you are now?

DAVID   *(Smiling)* The songs have helped me to put my focus where it needs to be—on God, and not on my circumstances!

REPORTER   Ah, yes, your circumstances...like when I met you before, in the wilderness, while you waited.

DAVID   *(Nodding)* Yes, I waited. I could have marched into Jerusalem and taken over, but I did not do that. I chose to trust God. His ways are perfect. He called me to be king, and while I waited for that to happen, I decided to sing to Him. I chose to have an attitude of gratitude and be thankful—no matter how things appeared to be. And, now, whenever I am in trouble, I still sing to the Lord, and He is still my hiding place!

Creative Illustration cont.
"David Sings Psalms"

DAVID'S SERVANT suddenly runs in, picks up David's "harp" and hands it to him.

SERVANT   King David! King David! The Philistine army is threatening to attack!

DAVID smiles as he takes the "harp" and puts his hand on the SERVANT'S shoulder. DAVID and the MAN both close their eyes and worship as David sings his response…REPORTER wipes tears from his eyes, obviously moved.

DAVID   The Lord is my hiding place; He will protect me from trouble and surround me with songs of deliverance. *(See Psalms 32:7 NIV)*

My soul finds rest in God alone; my salvation comes from Him. He alone is my rock and my salvation; He is my fortress, I will never be shaken. *(Psalms 62:1-2 NIV)*

DAVID and his SERVANT exit, still worshiping. **NOTE**: *This is real! Don't make fun here.*

REPORTER   *(Wiping more tears away.)* Well, folks, again today, we've just met with a king; actually, we have met with TWO kings! *(He looks up to Heaven and smiles; then exits.)*

IDE CLARE *(Enters wiping her eyes emotionally)* Hello, again children. Remember me? My name is Ide and my middle name is Clare—so I'm Ide Clare! That thare song of David's is found right here in the pages of God's Good Book, the Bible. Do you have one of these? Then look along with me at another place where David sang. It's found in Second Samuel 22…I'm going to read some of these to you and I'm going to SING them, because it says right here that David sang!

(IDE CLARE clears her throat dramatically and begins to sing the verses. DAVID comes and stands beside her, singing the same verses. Ide Clare looks up, surprised and pleased. She says, "Well, I declare!" and continues to sing the following selection of verses.)

(2 Samuel 22:1 NIV) David sang to the Lord the words of this song when the Lord delivered him from the hand of all his enemies and from the hand of Saul.

(2 Samuel 22:2 NIV) The Lord is my rock, my fortress and my deliverer;

(2 Samuel 22:3 NIV) My God is my rock, in whom I take refuge, my shield and the horn of my salvation. He is my stronghold, my refuge and my savior—from violent men You save me.

(2 Samuel 22:4 NIV) I call to the Lord, who is worthy of praise, and I am saved from my enemies.

(2 Samuel 22:7 NIV) In my distress I called to the Lord; I called out to my God. From His temple He heard my voice; my cry came to His ears.

Creative Illustration cont.
"David Sings Psalms"

(2 Samuel 22:17 NIV) He reached down from on high and took hold of me; He drew me out of deep waters.

(2 Samuel 22:18 NIV) He rescued me from my powerful enemy, from my foes, who were too strong for me.

(2 Samuel 22:47 NIV) "The Lord lives! Praise be to my Rock! Exalted be God, the Rock, my Savior!

(IDE CLARE and DAVID exit arm in arm, repeating 2 Samuel 22:47.)

ADVENTURES IN THE KINGDOM™
In Search of Wanderer Conclusion
"Singing to the Storm"

Creative Illustration 20 minutes

REVIEW THE STORY

PICTURE #1: "Seeker's Family"
Seeker and Moira's father's name was Wanderer. Wanderer used to live in the Kingdom… he used to live at home…but not anymore. Seeker and Moira were very sad.

PICTURE #5: "Seeker and Model Ship"
Seeker had made a special model ship at the Adventure Club.

PICTURE #19: "Seeker and the Broken Ship"
He put it in the stream to see if it would float, but began thinking about his father and forgot to watch it. It hit against some rocks and got broken.

PICTURE #21: "King Holding Seeker as He Cries"
Seeker cried to the King about his broken boat, and about his father.

PICTURE #22: "Broken Ship"
The King asked Seeker to give him the broken pieces and to REALLY trust him. The King said he could fix ANYTHING that has been broken.

PICTURE #32: "Through the Window"
Seeker and Moira went to the SECRET PLACE together to talk to the King about their father.

continued

Creative Illustration cont.
In Search of Wanderer Conclusion

PICTURE #3: "Royal Harbor"
Seeker and his friends went with Moira, Daring and the King out onto the open sea in the *Adventurer*.

PICTURE #35: "King on the Island"
The King took a rowboat and went in a disguise to the Island of Despair.

PICTURE #45: "Wanderer and the King"
Wanderer realized the King was the "Answer" and was set free from the dragons, Discouragement and Bitterness.

PICTURE #46: "The Storm"
Meanwhile, back on the ship, Moira, Daring, and the children were struggling to keep afloat. A raging storm had hit the Sea of Sadness. Winds of Weariness were blowing and waves were crashing against the ship with such force that it was difficult to keep standing.

Everyone was trying hard to overcome the sadness with gladness…they were walking around, holding onto the railing with big grins on their faces…but the storm just seemed too powerful.

"We've got to do something to calm the storm!" Moira shouted to Daring. "We must fight it together—we need a song!"

"A song?!" Daring echoed. "A song! Yes, a song!"

PICTURE #47: "On the Stormy Ship"
Daring shouted over the howling wind to the children, "Listen everyone, sing to the sadness! Sing songs you know and sing songs you make up!"

The children began to sing. Then Seeker made a discovery—he found that they could actually sing to the waves! He leaned over the side of the ship, chose a wave and called straight toward it, "Sing!" and the wave went down! Seeker leaned over the railing of the ship, aimed, and shouted, "Sing!" The wave went calm. The others were impressed. Soon everyone was using their songs to overcome the storm.

Seeker and Moira were standing together on the side of the ship, singing to the last few waves…"Sing!"…"Sing!" when Seeker looked off into the distance and suddenly cried, "Look! The King is coming back! The King is coming back!" Seeker looked more closely and caught his breath. "And….and…he's not…alone…!"

Everyone watched in silence as the rowboat came alongside the *Adventurer*. They watched as the King tied the boat securely to the ship and he and Wanderer climbed up the rope ladder.

continued

Creative Illustration cont.
In Search of Wanderer Conclusion

Then everyone stood back as Wanderer walked over to his children and stood silently in front of them. A moment of awkward silence passed, and then their father began to weep.

PICTURE #48: "Wanderer's Return"

"Moira…Seeker. I'm so sorry," he said, "I am so sorry. I never learned to overcome the obstacles in my life. Instead, I let the obstacles overcome me. Please, will you forgive me?"

Moira and Seeker nodded through their tears and rushed to put their arms around him. "We forgive you, Dad! We forgive you."

Their father hugged Moira and Seeker close and said, "The King has come to me, and he's given me a new heart, and a new name! From now on, I am Steadfast!"

As Moira and Seeker stood in their father's arms, Daring and the children happily gathered around and joined in for a group hug. Then Steadfast reached into a satchel and pulled out a polished wooden bow and five arrows with tiny blue and red feathers on the ends.

PICTURE #39: "Bow and Arrows"

Steadfast turned to Seeker and said, "I wanted to give these to you, son.

I've been working on this special set, and I was thinking about you the whole time while I worked. The King told me that you would REALLY like them."

"The King was right! Yes Dad, I REALLY like them! Thanks! Wow…these are nicer than any I've ever seen…"

PICTURE #49: "Steadfast, Moira, and Seeker"

Moira's eyes were shining. "Dad, it will be so good to have you back at home!"

"Well, Moira, the King and I talked about where I should live now. I'm back in the Kingdom, but I won't go home…not just yet…" Steadfast looked over at the King, who winked at him. "The King has given me a new name, but I need some time to grow into that name."

The King stepped forward. "Steadfast will stay in the castle with me for awhile, reading the Great Book and exploring. That way, he will grow stronger, and learn to overcome the obstacles he will face…"

"Before they overcome me!" Steadfast nodded. "I need to learn to be a good husband and a good father. I can't do it by myself."

Moira and Seeker were disappointed, but they understood. "Okay, Dad! We'll know right where to find you!"

continued

Creative Illustration cont.
In Search of Wanderer Conclusion

PICTURE #51: "Sunset"
Later, as the *Adventurer* sailed back toward Royal Harbor, the King smiled one of his mysterious smiles, and winked, motioning for Seeker to follow him. Everyone was so busy talking that they didn't notice the two of them slip up the stairs to the upper deck of the ship.

The sun was just starting to go down and the sky was full of beautiful colors. In the distance were the shores of the Kingdom. Seeker was sure that he could see his mother standing there, waving.

He waved back and turned excitedly to the King. "Wow! We sure have a surprise for her, don't we King!?"

"We sure do," agreed the King. "Oh, and Seeker, I want to give you something."

The King reached inside a pocket of his royal robe and pulled out…Seeker's model ship, perfectly mended and restored.

PICTURE #14: "Model Ship"
"Always remember, Seeker—I can put together anything that's been broken."

Secret Place Time 20 minutes

LEADER: When bad things happen in our lives…in our families, the King wants to help us. **He loves to fix things that are broken, especially broken hearts.** In the story, it looked like Seeker's broken family would be put back together…but listen, boys and girls…**Sometimes, broken homes and families just can't be put back together like they used to be**—people have remarried or moved away. Sometimes people who live in Despair want to STAY there—it's a choice they make. **But King Jesus certainly can put our hearts back together! He can make them even stronger than they were before the problem!**

Boys and girls, **even if your family is broken, King Jesus wants to heal your broken heart. Some things that have happened to you might be so bad that you will never forget them, BUT it doesn't have to hurt. Jesus wants to heal your pain.**

Let's go to the SECRET PLACE together right now and talk to the King…

"Hi, King Jesus. *(children echo)* I choose to trust You. *(children echo)* Help me to be like David *(children echo)* and continue to praise you, no matter what! *(children echo)* I choose to sing to my sadness *(children echo)* and I command the Winds of Weariness to stop blowing in my life!

Secret Place Time cont.

(children echo) Today I give you any broken pieces that are in my life *(children echo)* and I ask You to heal my heart. *(children echo)* Even if circumstances *(children echo)* can't be put back together *(children echo)* like they used to be *(children echo)* You can put my heart back together! *(children echo)* Thank You for the new song *(children echo)* the powerful song *(children echo)* that You have put into my heart. *(children echo)* Thank You, King Jesus, thank You. *(children echo)* Amen."

Boys and girls, **while we are here in the SECRET PLACE,** I want to invite you to ask the King to heal your heart. If you know what it's like to have a family member like Wanderer who left his family…we want to pray for you today. Or if someone close to you has really hurt you with what they have done or what they have said—**the King wants to heal your heart.**

Today, I want to do something different. **I want to sing a prayer over you.** Just like David sang his prayers, I want to sing a prayer over you. Psalms 32:7 says that the Lord surrounds us with songs of deliverance.

Invite the children to come and kneel at the front if they would like to. Have Small Group Leaders and other children come and pray with them. Be sensitive to the Lord and to the children. After an appropriate amount of time, quietly break into Small Groups while allowing those children who are still praying to continue to do so.

A PRAYER SONG OF DELIVERANCE *for you to use. Use a melodic voice to sing the following suggested prayer. It is meant only to be a starting place. Close your eyes and let the Holy Spirit sing through you a song of healing and deliverance for the children. You might also want to speak your prayer with worship music playing in the background.*

> Lord, I sing to the wounded hearts, to the lives that have been broken.
> I ask You, Lord, to heal these hearts from actions and words that were spoken…
> Rescue the children from the storms that life has brought upon them;
> Teach them to run with open arms to You, the One who loves them…
> Right here, right now, in the SECRET PLACE, wrap Your arms around them;
> Heal their hearts and ease their pain, Holy Spirit, comfort
> Comfort the children…Comfort the children… Comfort the children…
> And fill them full of Your Living Water; overflow them with Living Water.
> Overcome all of their sadness with gladness…
> Replace all their sadness with Your gladness, oh Lord.
> Surround them with songs of deliverance; songs of deliverance…
> Oh, children—Know that the Lord your God is with you!
> He is mighty to save. He will take great delight in you.
> He will quiet you with His love.
> He will rejoice, yes, He will rejoice over you with singing!
> Hear Him rejoice over you with singing…
> Right here, right now, in the SECRET PLACE.

Small Group Time

Small Group
10 minutes

Look up these verses and discuss what they mean in the lives of the children this week.

TODAY'S MEMORY VERSE: Psalms 42 - Sing to the sadness!
(The Psalms are songs!)

Psalms 32:7 - *He surrounds me with the song of deliverance.*
2 Samuel 22:1-50 - *David sang about God's deliverance.*
Psalms 33:3; 144:9; Isaiah 42:10; Revelation 5:9 - *Sing unto the Lord a NEW SONG.*
Psalms 41:5-9,13 - *David was in misery, yet he chose to sing praises to the Lord.*
Isaiah 61:1; Luke 4:18; Psalms 147:2 - *There is healing for broken hearts.*
1 Corinthians 14:15 - *Sing in the spirit and also with words you understand.*
Zephaniah 3:17 - *The Lord rejoices over us with singing!*

TALK ABOUT IT TIME
Discuss the following points from today's story:

- We have learned a lot the past few weeks about David. What was your favorite part of what we learned? Why?

- What was your favorite part of the Seeker story: *In Search of Wanderer*? Why?

- What was your favorite song? Why?

- What was your favorite memory verse? Why?

- What have you learned from this curriculum that will help you for the rest of your life?

SOMEONE IN THE BIBLE WHO SANG A NEW SONG
Psalms 32:7 - David was surrounded by songs of deliverance.

TOGETHER IN THE SECRET PLACE
(Not many adult prayers, please—let the children pray!)
Spend time praying for the upcoming FAMILY ADVENTURE.

DOOR HANGER

Duplicate for the children to cut out and take home. Encourage them to hang up this week's door hanger on their bedroom doorknob when they are spending time with King Jesus in the SECRET PLACE.

Shh! I'm with King Jesus in the Secret Place

MEMORY VERSES:
Psalms 42
(Hugga Wugga™ Paraphrase)

"I speak to the sadness in my heart—
'Hey, HEART! You believe!'
I'll read some verses from Psalm 42 and
I-WILL-SING!"

Seeker's SECRET PLACE

Week #12:
"Prayer-paration"
For Next Week's
Family Adventure

TODAY'S VERSE:
Psalms 40:1
(Hugga Wugga™ Paraphrase)

*"I waited hopefully for the Lord;
He turned toward me and
listened to my cry."*

Secret Sources of Power Quotes

Page 54 - From *Secret Sources of Power*

Are you prepared if God suddenly calls for an "audit" of your conduct toward your brothers and sisters? Remember that He doesn't need an audit—He already sees and knows all things. He holds each of us personally responsible for forgiving others, with no exceptions to the rule. We were not created or designed to carry bitterness and unforgiveness in our hearts. It is like trying to carry battery acid in a Styrofoam cup—the acid of unforgiveness eats away at every part of our lives.

Jesus said His disciples would be known for their love for one another. Love transcends the "ledger-sheet mentality" that keeps track of every wrong done and offense received. The "God-kind-of-love" described in First Corinthians chapter 13 doesn't keep a score or an "account" of wrongs suffered.

WEEK #12: "Prayer-paration"

Leader's "PRAYERparation"

Please take time to thoroughly read this lesson, as well as the front pages of this curriculum, well in advance of your teaching time.

Prayer-paration

Children in today's society often experience great pain. Even children from strong Christian families can accumulate a lot of disappointment and hurt feelings over the years. Sadly, much of the pain experienced in childhood is at the hand of parents. Sharp words or impatient actions from parents can deeply injure the children who love and trust them.

Please thoroughly read the section, FAMILY HEALING TIME, at the end of next week's FAMILY ADVENTURE outline. Let your PASTOR also read through it and get his blessing BEFORE you attempt to lead the people in this.

Foundational Scriptures for This Lesson. *Please Read Them...*

Romans 5:5 - *The love of God is poured out upon us.*
John 15:12 - *Love one another like Christ has loved you.*
Isaiah 61:1; Luke 4:18 - *Bind up the brokenhearted.*

Today's Verse:
Psalms 40:1 - *The Lord turned toward me and listened to my cry.*

Order of Activities (Suggested)

 5 min **Welcome**

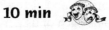 10 min **Creative Illustration**
Puppet show: "Whyatt and Whatson"

 45 min **Rehearsal for Family Adventure on Week 13**

 30 min **Small Group Time**

To maximize the effectiveness of this lesson, here is a
SUGGESTED LIST of materials:

• WHYatt and WHATson Puppets
• Party supplies if applicable
• **Basics** - Overhead projector, Transparencies, CD Player, Name tags, Bibles, Small Group Pages, Secret Place Doorknob Verse

WEEK #12: "Prayer-paration"

Leader & Small Group Leaders

IMPORTANT: Ask the Holy Spirit to HELP you so you can be patient, confident, and filled with joy while leading the children today in their rehearsal for the FAMILY ADVENTURE.

PRAY FOR THE CHILDREN before they come into the room today.

This prayer is taken from the song, "Mommy, I Need You" *(Track #6 on the CD)* and is based on Romans 5:5; John 15:12; Isaiah 61:1; Luke 4:18. Pray that the Holy Spirit will be Comforter and Healer in the midst of the families of your church fellowship.

"Jesus, I pray for our families
Pour out Your love in our homes
Help us to love each other
With the same kind of love you have shown.

Bind up the brokenhearted
Restore and renew and repair
Help us forgive each other
And heal every hurt…heal every hurt…heal every hurt
That's been there…"

Welcome
5 minutes

LEADER *(After welcoming the children)* We need the Holy Spirit to really HELP us get ready for next week's FAMILY ADVENTURE. I will explain how everything will work, then we will PRAY, and then we will rehearse the cheers, verses, and songs so that we can speak and sing with confidence! Boys and girls, we don't want to do some "cute" performance—we want to be POWER-FILLED ministers for King Jesus. And HE is the One we REALLY want to please.

Creative Illustration
10 minutes

"PUPPET SHOW: WHYatt and WHATson"
Have the same two puppets used previously in Week # 2—each wearing a name tag with their names printed in large bold letters: "WHYatt" and "WHATson." Use a puppet theatre or have the puppets behind a skirted table. WHATson carries a dictionary and speaks with a British accent. It would be fun to have him wear spectacles and a Sherlock Holmes hat. WHYatt is a typical young child who constantly asks "WHY?"

continued

Creative Illustration cont.
PUPPET SHOW: "WHYatt and WHATson"

LEADER	So, first we are going to rehearse ALL of our memory verses, cheers and songs.
WHYatt	*(Suddenly poking up from puppet theater)* WHY?
LEADER	Hello! I remember you!
WHYatt	*(Points to name tag)* My name is WHYatt! And my favorite thing to do is ask the question, "WHY"! So—WHY are you going to rehearse ALL of the memory verses, cheers and songs?
LEADER	Because next week is the FAMILY ADVENTURE!
WHATson	*(Suddenly poking up from puppet theater)* WHAT, may I ask, is a "FAMILY ADVENTURE"?
LEADER	Hello—I remember you, too!
WHATson	*(Points to name tag)* WHATson here! I am named that because my very most favorite thing to do is to ask the question, "WHAT"! So please, sir, tell me WHAT is a "FAMILY ADVENTURE"?
LEADER	Next week the children are going into the main sanctuary.
WHYatt	WHY?
LEADER	To do a presentation for the whole church! They will say all the verses and cheers we've been learning, and sing all the songs.
WHATson	So WHAT does all that have to do with a "FAMILY ADVENTURE"?
LEADER	After the children finish the presentation, we are going to have a special time for families to pray together.
WHYatt	WHY?
LEADER	Because families need to pray together.
WHATson	WHAT will they pray about?

continued

Creative Illustration cont.
PUPPET SHOW: "WHYatt and WHATson"

LEADER   They will pray about things we've learned in this curriculum—to run to the King in times of trouble, to choose to have an attitude of gratitude no matter what their circumstances, and to pour out their burdens in the SECRET PLACE!

WHYatt   WHY, I remember learning about burdens!

WHATson   I remember WHAT a burden is! I had looked it up in my handy-dandy dictionary! It is the best way I have found to learn more about WHAT I want to know! *(Flips through pages...)* Blessed...boxing...brother...Ah, here it is! *(Clears throat dramatically)* Burden: "something that is carried or endured with difficulty—like pain, shame, or guilt."

WHYatt   WHY would you want families to pray about burdens of pain, shame, or guilt? That doesn't sound like much of an adventure to me!

LEADER   Parents and children need to ask forgiveness of each other. They need to say they are sorry for words they've said and things they've done that caused pain. Then, when those burdens of pain, shame, and guilt are given up to King Jesus, He can fill the families with His love, joy, and peace!

                WHATson and WHYatt look at each other in silence.
                After a moment's pause they both nod in agreement.

WHATson   WHAT you are doing is a jolly good idea!

WHYatt   I don't know WHY you didn't do this sooner!

WHATson   Just think WHAT would happen if all the families of this church were emptied of their burdens and filled up full of Jesus' love! I say, carry on with the FAMILY ADVENTURE!

WHYatt and WHATson exit while WHYatt speaks. LEADER smiles and waves goodbye to them.

**Rehersal
45 minutes**

Rehearsal for the Family Adventure

LEADER

• Tell the children how next week's FAMILY ADVENTURE will work:

The children will go onto the platform and present the songs, cheers and verses *(as well as any skits or testimonies)*.

After that, they need to remain on the platform while you speak to the families; then the song, "Mommy, I Need You" will be played; then the children will go and pray with their families. Encourage the children to REALLY pray during this and to hug their parents and siblings; to really appreciate their families. Explain that if there are children in the group whose parents will not be in the meeting, they should stand with whoever brought them to church, or with their Small Group Leader.

• Spend time in prayer, letting the children pray for all aspects of the presentation. Also take time to pray for any children who are doing solos or testimonies. **Read Psalms 40:1 aloud and ask the Lord to turn toward you and hear your cries to Him on behalf of next week's service.**

• Then do a quick rehearsal of the following suggested outline, taking extra time on any weak areas. Insert into the outline any skits or testimonies you are planning and also rehearse them. Please refer to suggested order of events on next page.

**Small Group
30 minutes**

Small Group Time

TOGETHER IN THE SECRET PLACE
Overcome obstacles with opposites right now! Have one child at a time talk about an obtacle or problem they are facing. Have the other children give suggestions how to overcome the obstacle with an opposite. Then pray that the child will be able to overcome the obstacle.

There is a crossword puzzle to copy and send home or do together as a group.

Have a PARTY!

See PARTY SUGGESTION PAGE in the front section of the binder. If you will not have time in your meeting today for this, use the ideas at a later time.

© 2003 Dian Layton

FAMILY ADVENTURE
SUGGESTED ORDER OF EVENTS:

SONG: **"In the Secret Place"** (Track #1)

> **WEEK #1:** Psalms 91:1; Matthew 6:6
> **WEEK #2:** Matthew 11:28

SONG: **"More, More, More"** (Track #2)

CHEER: **"Unloading"**

> **WEEK #3:** Hebrews 12:1
> **WEEK #4:** Matthew 6:12, 14-15; Ephesians 4:32

SONG: **"The Holy Spirit"** (Track #3)

> **WEEK #5:** John 7:38-39
> **WEEK #9:** Romans 8:26-27

CHEER: **"Attitude of Gratitude"**

SONG: **"I'm Loved by God"** (Track #4)

> **WEEK #6:** Philippians 4:6
> **WEEK #7:** Psalms 61 and 62
> **WEEK #8:** 1 Peter 5:7
> **WEEK #10:** Romans 12:21
> **WEEK #11:** Psalms 42

SONG: **"He Is My Hiding Place"** (Track #5)

Seeker's SECRET PLACE
Crossword Puzzle

© 2003 Dian Layton

Seeker's SECRET PLACE
Crossword Puzzle

ACROSS
1. Seeker's mother
2. Overcome obstacles with -
3. Have an attitude of -
4. What to be filled up with
5. Wrap me up in Your…"
6. Seeker's sister
7. What He will give you when you come to Him

DOWN
1. Who you are loved by
2. He sang the Psalms
3. The Holy Spirit will teach you how to do this
4. The Holy Spirit is my -
5. Jesus is the -
6. The Island where Wanderer lived
7. What to do when someone hurts you
8. What to be emptied of
9. Wanderer's new name
10. Go there every day

DOOR HANGER

Duplicate for the children to cut out and take home. Encourage them to hang up this week's door hanger on their bedroom doorknob when they are spending time with King Jesus in the SECRET PLACE.

Shh! I'm with King Jesus in the Secret Place

MEMORY VERSE:
Psalms 40:1
(Hugga Wugga™ Paraphrase)

*"I waited hopefully for the Lord;
He turned toward me and
listened to my cry."*

Week #13:
"A Family Adventure"

From "Mommy, I Need You"
"Jesus, I pray for our families
Pour out Your love in our homes
Help us to love each other
With the same kind of love you have shown.

Bind up the brokenhearted
Restore and renew and repair
Help us forgive each other
And heal every hurt…
heal every hurt…heal every hurt
That's been there…"

Secret Sources of Power Quotes *(Re-emphasizing quote from Week 12)*

Page 54 - From *Secret Sources of Power*

Are you prepared if God suddenly calls for an "audit" of your conduct toward your brothers and sisters? Remember that He doesn't need an audit—He already sees and knows all things. He holds each of us personally responsible for forgiving others, with no exceptions to the rule. We were not created or designed to carry bitterness and unforgiveness in our hearts. It is like trying to carry battery acid in a Styrofoam cup—the acid of unforgiveness eats away at every part of our lives.

Jesus said His disciples would be known for their love for one another. Love transcends the "ledger-sheet mentality" that keeps track of every wrong done and offense received. The "God-kind-of-love" described in First Corinthians chapter 13 doesn't keep a score or an "account" of wrongs suffered.

WEEK #13: "A Family Adventure"

Suggested Order of Events

🎵 **SONG: "In the Secret Place" (Track #1)**

> **WEEK #1: Psalms 91:1; Matthew 6:6**
> **WEEK #2: Matthew 11:28**

🎵 **SONG: "More, More, More" (Track #2)**

CHEER: "Unloading"

> **WEEK #3: Hebrews 12:1**
> **WEEK #4: Matthew 6:12, 14-15; Ephesians 4:32**

🎵 **SONG: "The Holy Spirit" (Track #3)**

> **WEEK #5: John 7:38-39**
> **WEEK #9: Romans 8:26-27**

CHEER: "Attitude of Gratitude"

SONG: "I'm Loved by God" (Track #4)

> **WEEK #6: Philippians 4:6**
> **WEEK #7: Psalms 61 and 62**
> **WEEK #8: 1 Peter 5:7**
> **WEEK #10: Romans 12:21**
> **WEEK #11: Psalms 42**

🎵 **SONG: "He Is My Hiding Place" (Track #5)**

WEEK #13: "A Family Adventure"

FAMILY PRAYER TIME in the SECRET PLACE

The children remain on the platform while the LEADER speaks; then they will be directed to go and stand with their parents or whoever brought them to church.

LEADER

In this curriculum we have learned to run to the King in times of trouble; to pour out our burdens in the SECRET PLACE—to give King Jesus all of our sin, pain, shame, and guilt; our fears, and worries and disappointments. We've learned to forgive people who have hurt us with their words and actions. We've learned to choose to have an attitude of gratitude no matter what our circumstances; and we have learned that the Lord rejoices over us with songs of joy. He surrounds us with songs of deliverance.

Children in today's society often **experience great pain**. Even children from strong Christian families can accumulate a lot of disappointment and hurt feelings over the years. **Many of us adults have needed to receive healing from the Lord for childhood pain.**

Look at these children. Much pain has been healed during the past weeks as they met with King Jesus in the SECRET PLACE. **Our prayer is that they will DO what they have learned and continue to walk in forgiveness and healing into their adult lives.**

But right here, right now, we would like to take all of you **adults with us into the SECRET PLACE of His presence**…and receive His healing for you personally and for your family. Moms and Dads, please listen to me. **Sadly, much of the pain experienced in childhood is at the hand of parents. Our sharp words or impatient actions can deeply injure the children who love and trust us.**

Right now, we are going to listen to a **recorded song called, "Mommy, I Need You."** Please open your heart and listen to it as though your own child was singing it to you. Near the end of the song, the children will very quietly come to stand beside you and we will pray. **We will pray together and ask King Jesus to bring His healing presence into every home and every relationship.**

FAMILY PRAYER TIME
n the SECRET PLACE cont.

 RECORDED SONG: "Mommy, I Need You"

During the last part of the song, have the children very quietly go to stand with their parents. Then make sure everyone is with any family members who are present (Example: get the teenagers from the sound booth: make sure the pastor is with his family, etc) Encourage people who are by them-selves today to get adopted into a family near them; or to reach out their hands and pray for the families nearby.

Here is a suggested prayer to lead the congregation in.

 LEADER:

Please turn to the members of your family and say the following things after me:

> Hi!
>
> I'm so glad that God gave you to me.
>
> I want to ask your forgiveness.
>
> Please forgive me for all the times I have hurt you.
>
> Please forgive me for the words I have spoken that were cruel and sharp.
>
> Please forgive me for my impatient actions.
>
> I'm so sorry.
>
> I love you.
>
> I'm so glad that God gave you to me.
>
> Please pray for me. I need His help to be a better parent
> *(son, daughter, wife, husband).*

 RECORDED SONG: "Mommy, I Need You"

Play this softly again in the background and encourage families to continue talking and praying for each other for as long as possible. Don't be in a hurry.

 SONG: "In the Secret Place"

Put the words up for the congregation and finish the meeting with this song and a closing prayer from the LEADER.

SUGGESTION: At the end of today's meeting, have a catered FAMILY LUNCHEON for your church fellowship. *(Choose a simple, inexpensive meal like lasagna and salad.)* The goal would be to supply FAMILY time—so you would want to avoid having the moms in the kitchen! Please see the FRONT PAGES of this curriculum for more suggestions.

Songs and Cheers

PROCEDURES FOR CD

The process:

1) Download the CD content from its location on the web:
http://www.destinyimage.com/ygc

These files are organized by volume.
Please download the files which accompany this volume.
It is recommended that you download the files to your desktop.
Locate and double click the file icons on your desktop.

2) In order to open the .pdf files and view their contents, double click the file icons and they will automatically load in **Adobe Acrobat Reader**. If you know you don't have this program on your system, or you get a message from your computer asking which program you wish to use to view this file, then you will have to install **Adobe Acrobat Reader**. You can install this program simply and quickly by visiting the Adobe Website: http://www.adobe.com/products/acrobat/readstep2.html

Please feel free to do so at this time.

3) In order to hear the audio portion of this CD while viewing the contents of the accompanying .pdf file, follow these steps.
    a) Press the START button
    b) Go to **Programs➔Accessories➔Entertainment➔CD Player**
    c) Click on CD player, then double-click to open the audio file you have down loaded from the website and the music will begin to play.

4) Printing the transparencies: only certain pages are in full color. You can print these on transparency stock or regular paper stock from your color printer. With the file open, click print and select the page range you wish to print.

Curriculum #4 CD - Track Numbers

SONGS

Track #1:   In the Secret Place

Track #2:   More, More, More of Your Spirit

Track #3:   The Holy Spirit Song

Track #4:   I'm Loved By God

Track #5:   He is My Hiding Place

Track #6:   Mommy, I Need You

*NOTE: This song is only intended to be played during the FAMILY PRAYER TIME in Week #13. It is not intended as a song for the children to learn, so it is not included in the overhead transparencies or music sheets.

CHEERS

Track #7:   Unloading Cheer

Track #8:   Attitude of Gratitude Cheer

MEMORY VERSES (Hugga-Wugga™ Paraphrase)

Track #9: WEEK #1: Psalms 91:1-2; Matthew 6:6

Track #10: WEEK # 2: Matthew 11:28

Track #11: WEEK # 3: Hebrews 12:1

Track #12: WEEK # 4: From Matthew 6; Ephesians 4:32

Track #13: WEEK # 5: John 7:38-39

Track #14: WEEK # 6: Philippians 4:6

Track #15: WEEK # 7: Psalms 61 and 62

Track #16: WEEK # 8: 1 Peter 5:7

Track #17: WEEK # 9: Romans 8:26-27

Track #18: WEEK # 10: Romans 12:21

Track #19: WEEK # 11: Psalms 42

In the Secret Place

Dian Layton

**In the Secret Place
I will seek Your face
I will pour out my
heart to You**
In the Secret Place
I will sing Your praise
I will bow down and worship You
In the Secret Place
Each and every day
It's what I love to do
'Cause the Secret Place
Is my special place
To spend some time with You.

In the Secret Place, Page #2

He who dwells in the secret place of the Most High shall abide under the shadow of the Almighty. I will say of the Lord, "He is my refuge and my fortress; My God, in Him I will trust."

(Psalms 91:1-2 NKJV)

When you pray, go into your room, and when you have shut your door, pray to your Father who is in the secret place; and your Father who sees in secret will reward you openly.

(Matthew 6:6 NKJV)

More, More, More

Dian Layton

I'm wanting more, more, more
of Your Spirit;

I'm wanting more, more, more
of Your—life in me!

I'm wanting more, more, more
of Your power

And I'll get more of You
by giving up more of me!

Giving up more of me—
and letting You be

Ruler and King of my heart!

Giving up more of me—
and letting You be

Lord and Master of all…

"More, More, More" Page #2

CHORUS

So I will run to You when I'm worried

I will run to You when I'm afraid

When I need more strength in a hurry

I will run into the Secret Place

The Holy Spirit Song

Dian Layton

The Holy Spirit is my - TEACHER!

The Holy Spirit is my - HELPER!

The Holy Spirit is my COMFORTER…

Wrap me up in Your Presence, oh God.

Wrap me up in Your Presence, oh God.

Wrap me up in Your Presence;

Wrap me up in Your Presence;

Wrap me up in Your Presence, oh God.

"The Holy Spirit Song," Page #2

VERSE #1:

The Holy Spirit will help me when I PRA - AY!

The Holy Spirit knows exactly what to SAY - Hey, hey, hey!

VERSE #2:

The Holy Spirit will show me what I need to KNO - OW!

The Holy Spirit will show me the way to GO - Oh, oh, oh!

I'm Loved by God!

Dian Layton

When things go wrong

I sing this song:

I'm loved by God!

I'm not depressed or worried or stressed

I'm loved by God!

In every circumstance

I always have the chance

To focus on the fact

That I am loved by God!

"I'm Loved by God," Page #2

When things go wrong

I sing this song:

I'm loved by God!

I'm not depressed or worried or stressed

I'm loved by God!

Nothing can aggravate me

Or intimidate me

Nothing can separate me

From the love of God!

He Is My Hiding Place

Dian Layton

The Lord is my Shepherd and Helper

The Lord gives me songs in the night

The Lord is my Papa, my Father

He is the King of my life.

I run to His arms when I'm troubled

In His arms I am safe

He will keep me

Close–and not leave me

He is my Hiding Place.

"He Is My Hiding Place,", page #2

I tell Papa God how I'm feeling

I tell Him my worries and fears

I tell Him my secrets and wishes

And my Papa God always hears.

I run to His arms when I'm troubled

He holds me and kisses my face

Soon all my tears are gone

All of my fears are gone

He is my Hiding Place.

(Repeat all)

Unloading Cheer

Jesus took my burdens

He TOOK away ALL my sin!

Jesus took my burdens

My pain and shame and guiltiness!

Emptied of my burdens—
Filled up full with Jesus' love!

Emptied of my burdens—
Filled up full with Jesus' love!

I'm filled up full with Jesus' love!
I'm filled up full with Jesus' love!

Unloading Cheer, page #2
*Please Note: This verse is not on the CD—
follow the same rhythm*

Troubles, fears and worries

Disappointments—when they come

I GIVE them all to Jesus

And TAKE more of His love!

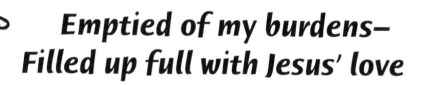

Emptied of my burdens—
Filled up full with Jesus' love

Emptied of my burdens—
Filled up full with Jesus' love

I'm filled up full with Jesus' love!
I'm filled up full with Jesus' love!

Attitude of Gratitude Cheer

Attitude of gratitude–a thankful heart

Attitude of gratitude–a thankful heart

Attitude of gratitude–a thankful heart

Attitude of gratitude–a thankful heart

Overcoming obstacles with opposites

Overcoming obstacles with opposites

Overcoming obstacles with opposites

Overcoming obstacles with opposites

Attitude of Gratitude Cheer, page #2

You overcome evil with–Good!

You overcome darkness with–Light!

You overcome greed with–Giving!

You overcome sadness with– Gladness–ALL RIGHT!

You overcome grumbling and complaining with

A VERY thankful heart!

The Secret Place

More, More, More Of Your Spirit

More, More, More Of Your Spirit   page 2

More, More, More Of Your Spirit page 3

I will run to You when I'm a - fraid.

When I need more strength in a hur - ry

I will run in-to the Se - cret Place.

D.S. al Fine

The Holy Spirit Is My...

The Holy Spirit Is My... page 3

I'm Loved By God

© 2003 Dian Layton

I'm Loved By God page 3

loved   by   God   When things go wrong   I

song   this song: I'm   loved   by   God!

I'm   loved   by   God!

© 2003 Dian Layton

He Is My Hiding Place page 3

© 2003 Dian Layton

Transparencies

"Seeker's Family"   Picture #1

"Daring"   Picture #2

© 2003 Dian Layton

"Royal Harbor"   Picture #3

MercyPlace Ministries

"Kingdom Kids"   Picture #4

"Seeker and Model Ship"   Picture #5

"Moira"   Picture #6

"Doodle and Do's Sailor Jig"   Picture #7

"Lantern"   Picture #8

"King"   Picture #9

"In the Cave"   Picture #10

"Darkness"   Picture #11

MercyPlace Ministries

"King Sitting"   Picture #12

© 2003 Dian Layton

"Hand on Heart"   Picture #13

"Model Ship"   Picture #14

"Trees and Scenery"   Picture #15

MercyPlace Ministries

"Stream"   Picture #16

© 2003 Dian Layton

"Clouds"   Picture #17

"Cloud Ship"   Picture #18

"Seeker and the Broken Ship"   Picture #19

"King at the Stream"   Picture #20

"King Holding Seeker As He Cries"   Picture #21

MercyPlace Ministries

"Broken Ship"   Picture #22

"Moira and Seeker on the Doorstep"   Picture #23

"Moira and Seeker"   Picture #24

© 2003 Dian Layton

"Window of the Secret Place"   Picture #25

"Stars"   Picture #26

"Stormy Ocean"   Picture #27

MercyPlace Ministries

"Darkness" Picture #28

"Lantern"   Picture #29

"Wanderer on Chair"   Picture #30

"Dragons!"   Picture #31

MercyPlace Ministries

"Through the Window"   Picture #32

"The Great Book"   Picture #33

MercyPlace Ministries

"The King's Wink"   Picture #34

"King on the Island"   Picture #35

"Sign: WANDERER'S WOODWORKING"   Picture #36

"Inside the Store"   Picture #37

MercyPlace Ministries

"Chained Dragons"   Picture #38

"Bow and Arrows"   Picture #39

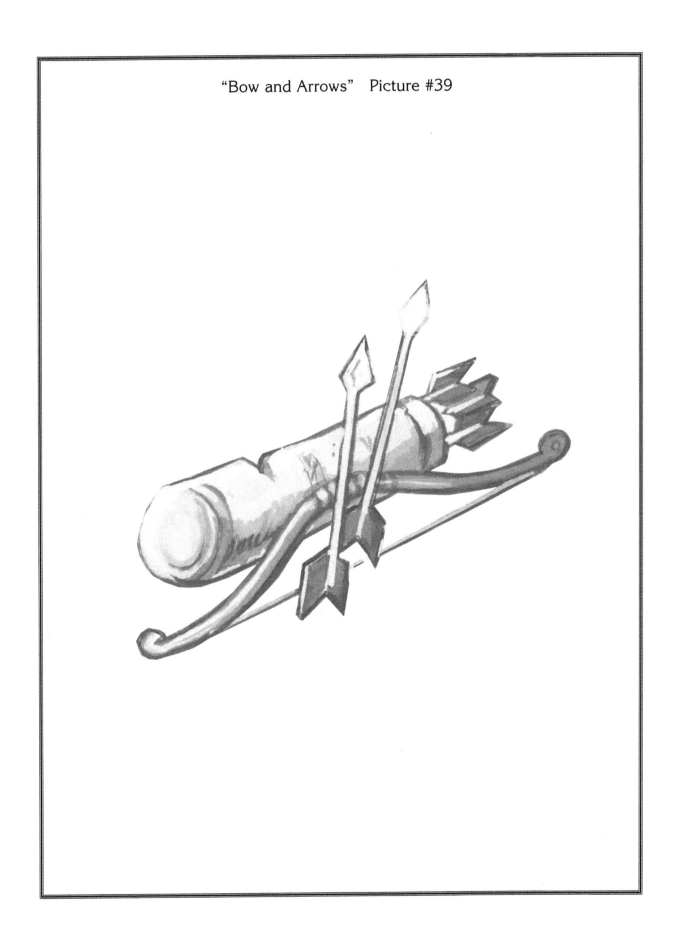

MercyPlace Ministries

"Wooden Castle"   Picture #40

"Bow and Arrow" Picture #41

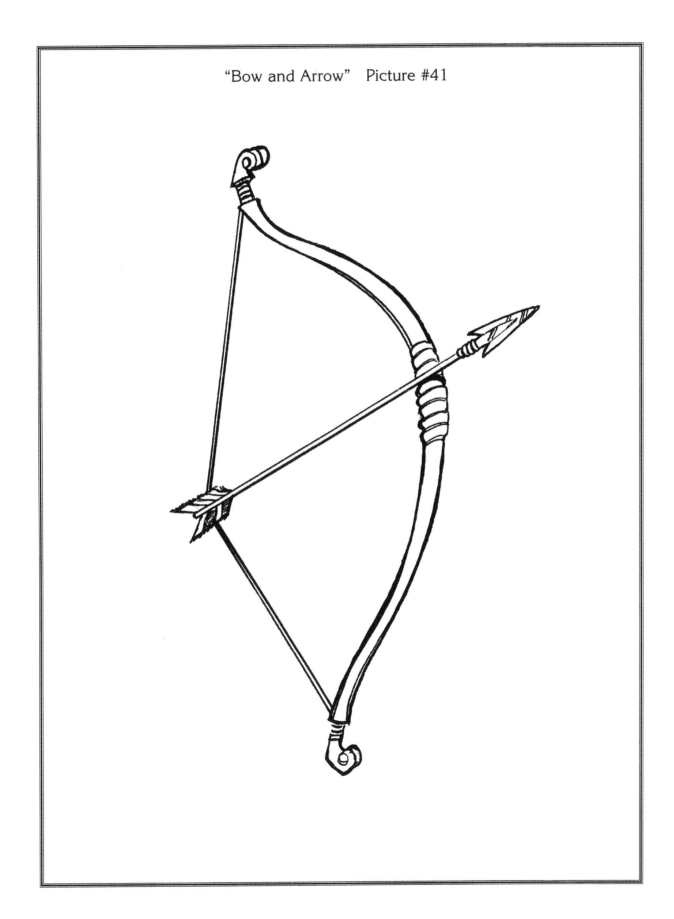

"The Great Book"   Picture #42

"Jesus on the Cross"   Picture #43

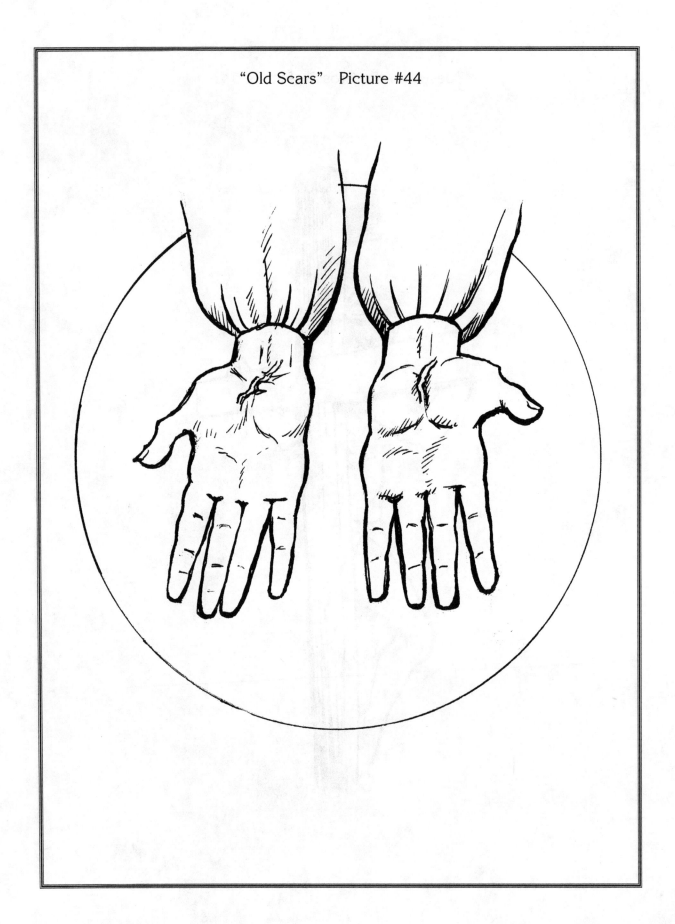

"Old Scars"   Picture #44

"Wanderer and the King"   Picture #45

"The Storm"   Picture #46

"On the Stormy Ship"   Picture #47

"Wanderer's Return"   Picture #48

"Steadfast, Moira, and Seeker"   Picture #49

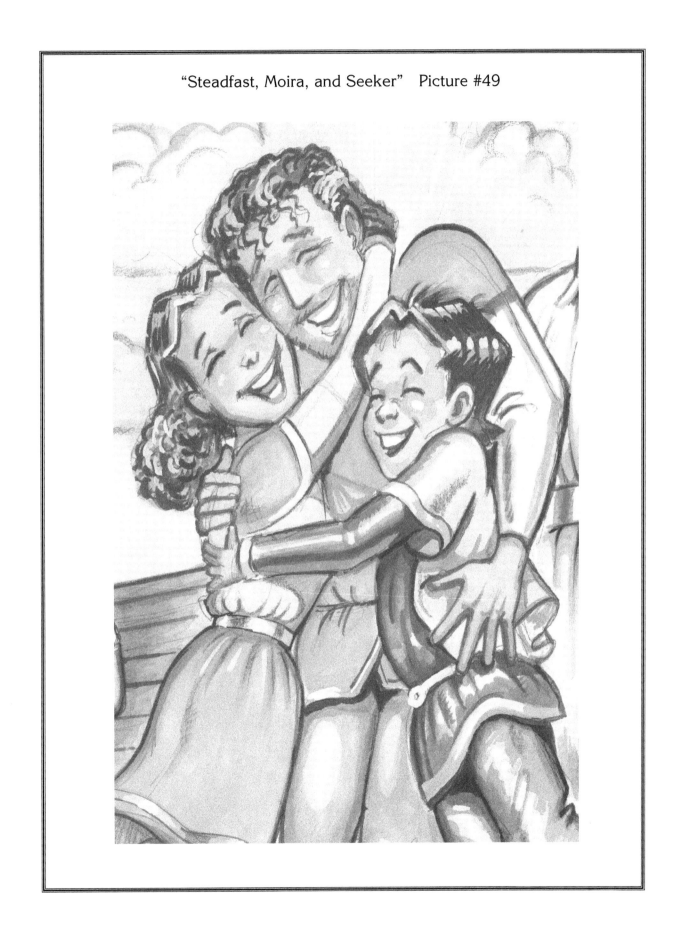

"Bow and Arrows"   Picture #50

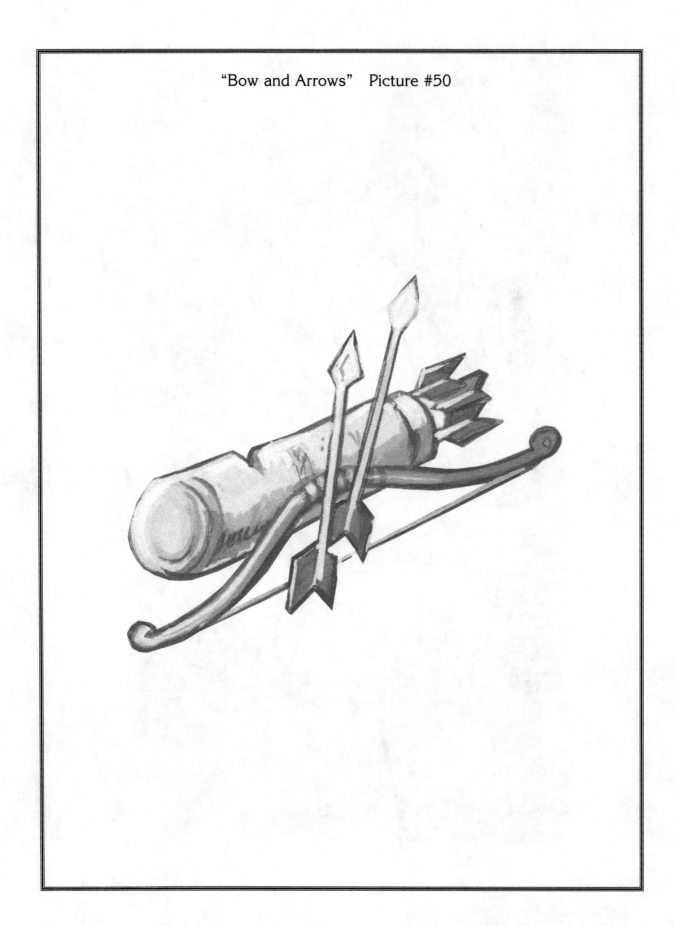

"Sunset"   Picture #51

"Model Ship"   Picture #52

CPSIA information can be obtained
at www.ICGtesting.com
Printed in the USA
LVHW051554140121
676460LV00016B/803

9 780970 791924